# FEMININE MULTIPLICITY

A Study of
Groups of multiple Goddesses
In India

SRI GARIB DASS ORIENTAL SERIES No. 207

# FEMININE MULTIPLICITY

## A Study of Groups of multiple Goddesses In India

Yoshinori Onishi

**Sri Satguru Publications**
*A Division of*
**Indian Books Centre**
**Delhi-India**

*Published by :*
**Sri Satguru Publications**
*A Division of :*
**Indian Books Centre**
Indological and Oriental Publishers
40/5, Shakti Nagar,
Delhi-110007
(INDIA)



**ISBN 81-7030-513-6**

**First Edition : Delhi, 1997**

Published by Sunil Gupta for Sri Satguru Publications a division of Indian Books Centre, 40/5, Shakti Nagar, Delhi-110 007, India and printed at D.K.Fine Art Press, Delhi-110 0052

## ACKNOWLEDGEMENTS

I should like to thank Dr David Smith, who gave me the opportunity to work on the fascinating topic of feminine multiplicity in Hinduism. He also directed me towards some very useful material and made a number of helpful suggestions. I wish also to acknowledge the help of Teru, my wife, who has given me constant encouragement and offered many insights, which have deeply influenced this work.

# CONTENTS

# CONTENTS

## ABBREVIATIONS

| | |
|---|---|
| DM | *Devī-māhātmya* |
| Mbh | *Mahābhārata* |
| RV | *Ṛgveda* |
| SB | *Śatapatha-Brāhmaṇa* |
| SV | *Sāmaveda* |
| TS | *Taittirīya Saṃhitā* |

# INTRODUCTION

The aim of this study is to examine into the meanings and significance of the multiplicity of the feminine in Indian subcontinent as exemplified by the 'Saptamātṛkās', the 'Nine Dūrgās', the 'letters of the Sanskrit alphabet (*mātṛkās*, "little mothers")', and so on. I refer to female deities that seem to function almost always as a group. It is as a group that these deities are considered significant and expounded in the texts. Questions that I discuss include: Are there any symbolic meanings in the numbers that are associated with the female deities? and Why are the prominent groups of multiple deities in India *feminine*, rather than *masculine*? It is true that groups of male gods are also found in Hinduism. Multiple male deities, however, do not appear to have been objects of major cults nor frequent motifs of iconography, as much of feminine multiplicity evidently was and, to a certain extent, still is.

It is not as if groups of multiple feminine deities had not yet been studied. For instance, a few detailed studies (e.g. Harper 1977; much of Tiwari 1985) have already been made in regard to the Saptamātṛkās, the most famous of the groups of goddesses concerned here. The Sixty-four Yoginīs have been the subject of a monograph (Dehejia 1986) and of a brief book (Das 1981). The 'letters/little mothers (*mātṛkās*)'—apart from a short book on the subject (Aryan 1980)—have been dealt with, though mostly briefly, in many studies concerned with particular aspects of Hindu Tantrism. The Seven Sisters have been described in studies of folk religion (e.g. Elmore 1913; H. K. Sastri 1974; Whitehead 1921). Thus, different groups of multiple goddesses have, individually, been studied by some scholars. And yet the question of feminine multiplicity as a whole, incorporating its various manifestations, does not seem to have received attention that it deserves. Part of the objective of publishing the present study is to rectify this situation. The relevance of this undertaking in the context of Indology will, I hope, become clear in what follows.

But first, I do, of course, have to delimit the scope of my study. Hinduism involves numerous groups of female deities (as noted by, e.g., Goudriaan 1979, pp. 64–66; Tiwari 1985, pp. 2–4, 10–17; Bhattacharyya 1974, pp. 104–07, 136; H. K. Sastri 1974, pp. 187–89). I have, however, chosen to deal primarily with the following groups: the Saptamātṛkās, the Seven Sisters, the Sixty-four Yoginīs, the 'letters', the Twelve Kālīs, the deities of the Śrī-Cakra, the Nine Dūrgās, and the Ten Mahāvidyās—for these groups seem to receive considerably more attention from the Hundus than do the ones left out and, further, these groups, taken together, constitute a fairly well-balanced amalgam involving a variety of aspects of Hinduism.

This study falls into two parts. Part I looks separately at different groups of goddesses, since it is necessary—before I can discuss feminine multiplicity as a whole—to define some of the most prominent manifestations of feminine multiplicity and to explore into the meanings of multiplicity in the context of each individual group. To do this effectively, I consider each group by presenting a brief general description of the group, by studying the group's relationship with male deities (if any is associated with the worship of the group), by examining the mode and aim of worship or other practice pertaining to the group, and then by summarizing the meaning of multiplicity involved in the group. The individual treatments of various groups of goddesses will, however, leave many issues unsolved, as I have implied above.

Part II, then, will aim at answering such unresolved questions. It will investigate feminine multiplicity as a whole, though bearing in mind its different manifestations such as will be considered in Part I, of course. Part II will search a variety of sources for clues to explaining the phenomenon of feminine multiplicity in Hinduism. Particularly, I shall draw on literary, mythological, anthropological, and psychoanalytical evidence regarding the Indian perception of women.

One of the limitations of this study is that I am not a Hindu myself. A Japanese born and raised in Japan, I come from a cultural system that is totally different from the cultural system in which the subject matter of this study is located. This represents a limitation to the access I have, particularly, to the inner aspects of the Hindu feminine multiplicity, such as the feelings the Hindus may have towards the feminine. Another limitation I should mention here is the fact that I am not a woman. Though discussions with my wife have furnished many insights empowered by her feminine instincts, I, the author, have no direct access to feminine instincts. This is perhaps not a major obstacle since the present study is largely concerned with the *perception* of women, as opposed to *women's* perception of things. Still, this is a limitation that I wished to make clear. It is, then, with an awareness of these limitations, among others, that I have undertaken this study.

# PART I

I begin with a preliminary note on the way in which I have arranged the first four chapters of Part I. These four chapters are all connected, in one way or another, with the concept of the Saptamātṛkās. Though the beginnings of the Saptamātṛkās do not seem very clear, it may be possible to hypothesize that the following three groupings have all played some role or other in the formation of the concept of the Saptamātṛkās: viz. the groups of seven/six figures represented in some of the seals from Indus Valley Civilization (Parpola 1985, Fig. 33 and 34), many female heptads appearing in the Vedas (e.g. the Seven Mothers of Soma, the Seven Rivers), and the Dravidian/aboriginal Seven Sisters/Virgins. If this hypothesis is correct, then an investigation of these three kinds of manifestations of feminine multiplicity is a prerequisite for understanding the full implications of the multiplicity that is found in the Saptamātṛkās. For this reason, chapters 1, 2, and 3, will deal with these three kinds of feminine multiplicity, respectively, and the Saptamātṛkās will be looked at in chapter 4. (More detailed arguments and supporting material regarding the formation of the Saptamātṛkās will be presented at relevant places below.)

In addition to making a contribution (if any) to the formation of the Saptamātṛkās, the three groupings—viz. the Indus Valley groups of seven/six figures, the Vedic female heptads, and the Dravidian Seven Sisters/Virgins—may have exercised influence upon one another, except that the Vedic heptads are not likely to have influenced the Indus seven/six figures, for that would be anachronistic. This hypothesized network of the exertion of influence, then, may be summarized as in the diagram below:

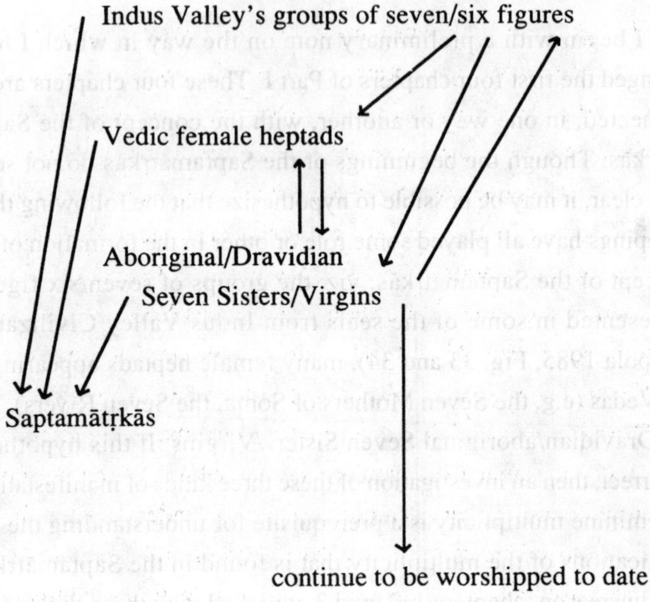


Before moving on to the next section, I should also mention that the Dravidian Seven Sisters/Virgins have further significance for us, quite apart from their proposed connections with the Saptamātṛkās. That is, the Dravidian Seven Sisters/Virgins have been of great importance in their own right and—unlike the Indus Valley groups of seven/six figures and the Vedic female heptads—are worshipped in Indian villages even today. The Saptamātṛkās themselves, incidentally, have long ceased to be the objects of major cults.

# 1. THE GROUP OF SEVEN/SIX FIGURES IN THE INDUS VALLEY CIVILIZATION

## 1.1 GENERAL DESCRIPTION

One of the seals that concern us here was found in Mohenjo-daro and shows a row of seven standing human figures in the lower register (Parpola 1985, Fig. 33). In the upper register, this seal shows a goddess in a pipal [fig tree] (*aśvattha*) (as recognizable from its leaves—Banerjea 1956, p. 168), a kneeling human figure in a supplicating gesture facing her, and, behind this kneeling figure, a human-faced goat (ibid.) with magnificent goat horns, also facing the goddess. There is also something that looks like a severed human head placed on a throne (Parpola 1985, p. 215) between the goddess and the kneeling figure. The goddess, unclothed, wears three horns (looking like the three points of a trident) on the head and a long mass of hair gathered at the back of her head. She also wears several bangles on both arms. Similar *triśūla* horns and hair-do appear on the kneeling figure. All human figures in this scene (except the severed head) are probably female, though some scholars dispute this, as summarized by Tiwari (1985, pp. 139–41).

The seven figures, all clad in a knee-length skirt, look identical. They all wear what most authors have regarded as a long pigtail decorated with leaves or feathers (e.g. Banerjea 1956, p. 168). They also wear what might be a pair of feathers or horns at the top of the head. The seven figures have been variously interpreted. Marshall interpreted them as 'female officiants or ministrants of the goddess' (quoted in Harper 1977, p. 9) performing some kind of ritual dance (Tiwari 1985, p. 139). Mackay, on the other hand, suggested on the basis of the number seven that these figures might be the goddess

Śītalā and her six sisters (ibid.). Analogy to other groups of seven goddesses found in Indian villages has been drawn by another scholar (Harper 1977, p. 9). A more Indo-Aryan kind of identification of the seven figures has been provided by Dhavalikar, who, on one occasion, explains this seal as a representation of a Ṛgvedic passage (9.102.4) in which the *sapta-mātaraḥ* are portrayed as regulating the preparation of Soma—the tree representing the Soma plant, the deity in it being the god Soma, and the kneeling figure being Agni (Tiwari 1985, p. 140). At another place, however, Dhavalikar identifies the seven figures in this seal as the 'proto-Saptamātṛkās' from whom the later concept of the Purāṇic Saptamātṛkās developed—an identification that is favoured by Harper (1977, p. 9).

On the other hand, Tiwari (1985), who has looked fairly extensively at various scholars' interpretations of the seven figures, seems to be among the most cautious concerning the identity of the seven figures. He says that 'the seal appears good evidence of worship of a tree-deity.... But to read more than this seems unwarronted (*sic*)' (Tiwari 1985, pp. 141–42). His primary reasons for this extreme scepticism are the following (ibid., pp. 141–43). (1) Other than the position of the tree deity, who is the principal figure, and the supplicating gesture of the kneeling figure facing the tree deity, this seal provides no evidence clear enough for any positive identification. (2) The Indus and the Vedic cultures were alien to each other. The latter, therefore, should not be read into the remains of the former. (3) Though there are several other seals depicting a group of seven human figures, 'not much should be made of the number seven ... for ... there is one seal impression with a representation very similar to the Mohenjodaro seal referred to but showing only six so-called "votaries" or "ministrants"' (ibid., p. 142).

Regarding his reason (1), I do agree that there is not a great deal of evidence here. But I feel that the right attitude to take for our purposes—viz. to understand the question of feminine multiplicity—is to look closely and carefully at every possible clue available. We should not dismiss any information too hastily.

I turn next to Tiwari's reason (3). First, in keeping with what I have just said about Tiwari's reason (1), the right attitude here would be to take the number seven more seriously than recommended by Tiwari, especially since there are several representations of a group of seven figures in the Indus Valley Civilization, as noted above (citing Tiwari). This amount of regularity seems significant. Secondly, it has been stated by Parpola (1985, p. 121) that the fluctuation between the numbers seven and six (appearing in very similar scenes—Parpola 1985, Fig. 33 and 34), itself, suggests that these figures may be the stars of the Kṛttikās (Pleiades), which are associated with the birth of the war-god Skanda, for in epic and Purāṇic mythology this group's members are either seven or six in number, depending on whether the chaste Arundhatī is counted or not. The Kṛttikās also appear in later Vedic literature. Parpola further identifies the severed head on the throne (about which nothing much has been said by any other scholar) as that of Skanda, the hair of the severed head arranged into a double bun at the back suggesting the Harappan warrior's hair-do (ibid., pp. 120–21). In the Mbh (3.215.13 ff), the gods' plot to kill this powerful war-god by means of Vāsava and all the Mothers of the World fails. Vāsava refuses to undertake the task of killing him, saying that Skanda is too powerful for him, while all the Mothers of the World—though initially having agreed to kill him—upon seeing him, went to him for refuge. Perhaps, it is not very likely for an Indus seal to represent an exact scene from later mythology. Yet, Parpola's proposed identification of the seven/six figures with the Kṛttikās is worth considering in more detail, for this constellation seems to have always been among the most noticeable and conveyed some important symbolical meanings to the ancient man throughout the world, as we shall see below. Further, while six of the stars of this constellation can be easily seen with the naked eye (third magnitude), the seventh can only be seen with strong eye-sight in very clear atmospheric condition (sixth magnitude) (Harper 1977, p. 44). In Greek mythology, too, 'the seventh Pleiad sometimes vanishes (often said to be the result of a sexual offense)' (O'Flaherty 1973, p. 100). I shall look at the Kṛttikās in more detail later.

Turning to Tiwari's reason (2), we see that it is based, partly, on Marshall's theory about how the Vedic and Indus Valley cultures were intrinsically alien to each other (Tiwari 1985, p. 142). More importantly, however, Tiwari's reason (2) appears to derive its force from a certain model of inter-cultural influence. Tiwari's argument is based largely upon the idea that the Vedic Aryans were partly or largely responsible for the disappearance of the Indus Valley Civilization—with the implication of the occurrence of supposedly inevitable hostile conflict between the two cultures. Tiwari claims that since neither the seven figures in the Indus seal nor the Vedic female heptads (Seven Mothers, Rivers, Rays, etc.) are portrayed as being of the nature of 'intruding elements' in the respective culture in which they are found (as Rudra-Śiva seems to be), the concept of seven female divinities cannot have been borrowed from one culture to the other (ibid., pp. 142–44). It follows, says Tiwari, that if the group of seven figures in the Indus seal under discussion is a representation of the Seven Mothers, then the same concept of the Seven Mothers would have to be indigenous to both cultures—but this 'is not possible to imagine' (ibid., p. 144). Here, Tiwari is rejecting two possible explanations of the existence of the concept of the seven divine females in the two cultures. One explanation is to say that the concept of a group of seven divine females was indigenous to the Indus Valley and adopted by the Aryans, and the other is to assume that this concept was originally known to both cultures. While I do not support Dhavalikar's particular Ṛgvedic identification (noted above), I think that Tiwari's way of rejecting those two explanations has some problems.

First, in regard to the idea of the Aryans being responsible for the disappearance of the Indus Valley Civilization, we have, in fact, no way of knowing whether or not any actual intercourse between the Indus and Vedic peoples even took place at all (Harper 1977, p. 16). The usually employed reasoning is as follows. By the middle of the second millennium BCE, the Indus cities seem to have been defunct, and the arrival of the Aryans in the Indus Valley is likely to have corresponded in date. It would, therefore, be logical to assume the Aryans' arrival to have been an important factor in the demise of the Indus Valley Civilization, given no evidence of any other factor. But in fact, there *is* precisely such evidence. Bryson (1989, pp. 300–01) has reconstructed a record of monsoon rainfall for the last 12,000 years, based on fossil pollen recovered from Lunkaransar Dry Lake in Rajasthan. His record shows that, compared with the present, there was a great deal of rain in that area for about seven thousand years beginning about 8500 BCE, but that the rains ceased almost completely in about 1600 BCE. His record shows that the monsoon failed for about 700 years. This long drought must, at least partly, account for the disappearance of the Indus Valley Civilization since its cities seem to have relied on 'the agricultural success of the outlying areas' (Harper 1977, p. 14). Regarding the Aryans' supposed connection, it is not impossible to imagine that they came to the Indus cities after the Indus culture had died out, especially because, even for nomads like the Aryans, the 700-year-long severe drought might not have been a favourable condition in which to invade and fight. If this line of conjecture is correct, it is not necessary to assume that there was hostile conflict between the Aryan and Indus peoples, as has often been believed.

On the other hand, if we suppose that there was some intercourse between the Indus and Vedic peoples, do we have to assume that there was hostility between them? Not necessarily, for by the time of the Aryan immigration, the afore-mentioned long drought might have weakened the Indus people sufficiently and made hostility between the two peoples unnecessary. Alternatively, if the Aryans arrived before the drought, we might assume that after a certain period of coexistence in the valley, the kind of culture that was dependent on the pre-drought climate was simply not able to survive, while the nomads' culture was. Regarding their coexistence, there is no intrinsic reason why the interaction between any two different cultures has to be hostile. That we feel that it has to be that way might be a result of our modern way of living. Two different cultures could be mutually enriching. Evidence presented by Harper's study (1977) also indicates that any interaction that might have taken place between the Indus and Vedic peoples was not nearly as hostile as generally assumed. It would appear, then, that we need not assume that anything borrowed from either culture into the other has to have a mark of being an 'intruding element'. It is true that there is a famous case of Rudra-Śiva, who is evidently seen by the Vedic writers with deep suspicion and who is very likely a non-/pre-Aryan god (Tiwari 1985, p. 143n280). Yet there is no evidence to prove that this god had no inauspicious aspect *in his indigenous culture* to begin with. He could have had both auspicious and inauspicious sides from the beginning. Besides, the *Ṛgveda* itself evidently contains adaptations from the non-Aryan indigenous culture that are not portrayed as inauspicious, or suspicious, intruding elements. The seven river goddesses called Saptasindhu are a case in point. They are not seen as inauspicious in any way but their names show that these are actual *Indian* rivers (Griffith 1963, Vol. I, p. 44n12).

I thus disagree with Tiwari's rejection of the first of the aforementioned two explanations of the supposed existence, in both the remains of the Indus vulture and the Vedic literature, of the concept of seven divine females. I do not reject the second explanation, either, viz. that this concept was familiar to both peoples prior to their supposed contact with each other—a theory rejected by Tiwari as not possible to imagine. This concept of seven divine females is not very straightforward and actually involves a number of concepts and ideas in complicated manners.

Yet, as far as the Kṛttikās (Pleiades) are concerned, Harper (1977, pp. 37–40) has demonstrated that many ancient cultures in the world imparted great significance to this constellation. Prior to Harper, Sir James Frazer, whose work she has drawn on, provided detailed descriptions (1933, pp. 307–19) of the central role played by the Pleiades in primitive calendars the world over. These stars were, most importantly, considered to mark the beginning of the year and to determine the seasons for planting and reaping. It should not be surprising, therefore, if we find that the Pleiades were of great significance also in the Indus calendar, agriculture, and religion. In Classical Greek culture, for instance, the reappearance of the Pleiades, known as the seven sisters there, seems to have marked the end and rebirth of one cyclic year, its risings and settings dividing the year into two alternating periods of warmth and cold, growth and dormancy, and so on (Harper 1977, pp. 39–40). Its reappearance was, in general, the harbinger of the growing season. Though now, in the Northern Hemisphere, the Pleiades appear on the horizon in May and disappear in late October or November (ibid., p. 38), the rising of this stellar grouping seems to have corresponded, around 2240 BCE, to the vernal equinox, which was traditionally regarded, in many cultures, as the beginning of the new year when the sun-rise defines due east (Parpola 1985, p. 100; O'Flaherty 1973, p. 100; Harper 1977, p. 38; Kane 1974, Vol. V, Part 1, pp. 507–08; cf. MacDonell & Keith 1967, pp. 421ff). Harper, further, says that Taurus—in which the Pleiades, perhaps Taurus's most conspicuous constituent (as a group), appear—which is traditionally the first sign of the zodiac in many cultures, is represented by the first letter of the Greek alphabet (*alpha*), of the Hebrew alphabet (*aleph*), and of the Hindu system (*a*) (1977, pp. 37–38). Primitive cultures in which the Pleiades were of great significance abound, and many examples (such as from South America) are also presented by Lévi-Strauss (1970, pp. 216–27). One more thing worth noting about the Pleiades is that, though we have been emphasizing the agricultural association of this constellation, the Pleiades received much attention even from savages who do not practise agriculture. For instance, the Australian aborigines apparently sang and danced in order to 'gain the favour of the Pleiades (*Mormodellick*), the constellation regarded as the giver of rain and even cursed if its appearance is not followed by the expected rains' (Frazer 1933, p. 307). To give another example, the Abipones of Paraguay, who did not till the ground, looked upon the Pleiades as an image of their ancestor, saluting the reappearance of this constellation with joyous shouts and music as their ancestor's yearly return (ibid., p. 308).

In summary, then, what we can say about the Indus seals' group (singular, because these groups seem to appear in variants of the same scene) of seven/six figures is this. Considering the important place given to the Pleiades in many primitive cultures throughout the world, we should not be surprised if the Indus group was the Kṛttikās, regardless of whether or not there was any interaction between the Indus and Vedic peoples. We have indications that the Pleiades' importance was acknowledged by the Vedic Aryans, as we shall see in the next chapter. If the Indus group of seven/six figures was also the Pleiades (Kṛttikās), and if there was interaction between the two cultures, then either the two cultures discovered upon contact that they had the concept of seven divine females in common (as suggested by Harper 1977), or the Vedic Aryans borrowed it from the Indus culture.

## 1.2 THE FEMALES' RELATIONSHIP WITH MALES

As I said in my Introduction above, I shall be looking—in regard to each main group considered in this study—at the group's relationship with the male(s), the mode and aim of worship, and the meanings of multiplicity. The present section is concerned with the relationship of the Indus seals' group of seven/six figures with males. As we have already noted, some scholars have seen a male human figure(s) in the main Indus seal under discussion (Parpola 1985,

Fig. 33). Dhavalikar and Wijesekera (Tiwari 1985, p. 141) have even considered the tree-deity to be male. Mitchiner (1982, p. 269) has identified the seven anthropomorphic figures with the 'seven sages'. Some have said that all human figures might be male (as noted by Tiwari 1985, p. 141). Nevertheless, as we have said above, the majority of scholars seem to regard all human figures in this seal as female.

This leaves us with little to say in this section, except that Parpola (1985, pp. 120–21) has suggested that the object in front of the supplicating figure is a severed human head placed on a throne and that the double-bun fair-style indicates that it belonged to a warrior (male). This object does look like something being offered to the tree-deity. Parpola (ibid.) suggests that this seal depicts a sacrificial scene in which the head, having been cut off from a warrior, is offered to the goddess of Victory inhabiting the sacred tree for the sake of victory. If this interpretation is correct, we might say that we have female superiority over males here, as far as the tree-deity is concerned. One problem, however, is that, although this seal seems to depict a religious scene, there is no agreement among scholars concerning its exact nature (Tiwari 1985, p. 139). Nevertheless, it is significant that no alternative view has so far been expressed regarding what Parpola sees as a severed human head on a throne.

What about the group of seven figures itself? Supposing Parpola's interpretation of the severed head is correct, does the fact that these seven figures share certain features with the tree deity enable them to partake of the tree goddess's superiority over the masculine? Their similarities include the following. First, all these figures are shown in the frontal position, with the head and feet facing to their right. Second, they all wear bangles on both arms. Third, looking at the heads of the seven figures, we see that their head-gear and hair-do (described above) show certain similarities to, as well as differences from, those of the tree-deity. Differences also include the fact that the seven figures wear a skirt, whereas the tree goddess is unclothed. Further, the tree goddess is being supplicated by the kneeling figure, while the role of the seven figures in this scene is not clear. There is, of course, Dhavalikar's aforementioned interpretation of this seal as a representation of a Ṛg-vedic passage in which the Seven Mothers are said to regulate the preparation of Soma. But this precise identification of the scene has not been accepted widely (cf. e.g. Tiwari 1985, p. 140). I have said above that the possibility of the Pleiades being known to the Indus culture need not be ruled out, and I shall, in chapter 2, consider the connection between the Pleiades and the Vedic concept of seven divine females (which involves the Seven Mothers). However, the seal under discussion simply does not provide enough information concerning the exact nature of the role played by the seven figures.

One more thing we may note in this section is the fact that, in comparison to the small number of male figures found in the Indus Valley Civilization, hundreds of female figurines have been discovered (Kinsley 1986, p. 214). This impressive number itself might, perhaps, suggest the greater significance of the feminine, at least in certain respects, than the masculine in this civilization. Though some male figures are quite dramatic and striking, so are some female figurines. It seems probable that goddesses were widely worshipped and exalted (Kinsley 1986, p. 219). (The nature of the goddesses will be treated in more detail in a later chapter.)

In sum, then, these numerous Indus figurines perhaps indicate the greater feminine significance, in certain respects, than the masculine in the Indus culture in general. In the main seal that I have discussed, we might have an instance of feminine superiority *in the tree goddess* over the masculine if Parpola's interpretation is correct. We are not certain, however, about the exact nature of the relationship of the Indus group of seven/six figures with male(s), other than the fact that they share certain features with the tree goddess.

## 1.3 MODE AND AIM OF WORSHIP/OTHER PRACTICE

Here again, we are not sure how, and for what reasons, the Indus seals' group of seven/six (whoever these figures might be) was worshipped. If we suppose that this group was the Krttikās, then it might have been connected, as we have suggested above, with the beginning of the year and of the growing season, etc. This group, then, might have been worshipped for the sake of fertility, for example. There are several seals from the Indus Valley Civilization that indicate that a goddess connected with vegetation was known (Kinsley 1986, p. 279). In addition, some seals show a female figure who may be associated with the fertility of animals (ibid.). These females, however, are presented as individuals, not as a group.

In regard to the mode of worship of our group of seven/six, we know even less. In religious setting generally, fertility is often connected with sacrifice, and some scholars have suggested that our main seal depicts a sacrificial scene. For instance, we have looked at Parpola's idea about the 'severed human head'. He further suggests that the human-faced goat is *śarabha*, the wild markhor goat, spoken of in the *Kālikā Purāṇa* as a sacrificial animal that pleases the Goddess as much as a buffalo does (1985, p. 121). As I have noted, however, there is no unanimity about the exact nature of the scene in question. Mackay even sees the goat as a form of the goddess herself—far from a sacrificial victim (Tiwari 1985, p. 139). Besides, most scholars who regard this scene as a sacrifice consider the victim(s) as being offered to the tree goddess, not to the seven figures; thus, their suggestions are relevant to us only to the extent that the group of seven figures partakes of the tree goddess's nature.

## 1.4 MEANING OF MULTIPLICITY

The assumption that the Indus seals' group of seven/six figures may be the Kṛttikās is essentially sound. Yet, it is not proven. At any rate, since the Kṛttikās are one of the important heptads in the Vedas, I shall discuss the meaning of this group's multiplicity in the next chapter, which is concerned with the Vedic female heptads.

# 2. VEDIC FEMALE HEPTADS

## 2.1 GENERAL DESCRIPTION

Chapter 2 attempts to find out what contribution, if any, was made by female heptads appearing in the Vedas towards the formation of the concept of the Saptamātṛkās. The extent to which these heptads are regarded as connected with the Saptamātṛkās, however, varies amongst scholars, two most important of whom must be Tiwari (1985) and Harper (1977). I shall look at this question in section 2.4 below, which will deal with the meaning of multiplicity that might be found in the Vedic female heptads. In the present section, I should like to give a brief description of prominent female heptads that feature in the Vedas.

First, I look at the early Vedic period. There are many references to female heptads in this period. But I shall restrict myself to ones that are the most prominent and, therefore, the most significant for us.

The first thing to be noted concerning those female heptads is that they may have been equated with one another. One aspect of their equation seems to be achieved through their association with Agni. This god's close association with female heptads has been pointed out by Harper (1977, p. 30). We read in the RV, for instance, that Agni was born 'in the waters ... with the Sisters' labour' (RV 3.1.3),[1] and these Sisters, or waters, are also referred to as 'the Seven Strong Floods', who augmented him (RV 3.1.4). The same hymn also portrays Agni as seeking, and being received by, 'heaven's

[1] Translations of all Vedic passages are by Griffith 1963 unless otherwise indicated. Identifying numbers of verses and notes correspond to those used by him.

Mighty Ones,' also called 'Seven Sounding Rivers' (RV 3.1.6). Another text, SV, incidentally, says that Agni was taught, at his birth, by his Seven Mothers in the ways of wisdom (SV 2.1.1.5, as noted by Harper 1977, p. 30). Returning to the RV, we see that Agni's home is in 'the seven auspicious Mothers' (RV 1.141.2). The RV places emphasis on Agni's seven rays, also referred to as seven tongues, flames, or reins (e.g. RV 1.105.9, 1.146.2, 9.102.2, 10.5.5, also 4.1.12 with n12, 4.7.5 with n5, 4.50.4 with n4). The seven tongues or flames of Agni are also called 'Seven red Sisters' (RV 10.5.5 with n5).

Like Agni, Soma also had Seven Mothers (RV 9.102.4), who are also referred to as the seven rivers or seven sister-streams (RV 9.66.8) or the seven sisters (RV Valakhilya.11.4). At Soma's birth, his Seven Mothers 'taught him, for glory' (RV 9.102.4).

Whether explicitly connected with Agni or Soma, many references seem to equate the Seven Mothers with the seven rivers (e.g. RV 8.85.1), with the waters (RV 10.30.10), and with the seven sisters (e.g. RV 9.86.36). The seven sisters themselves in turn seem to be equated with the seven rivers which not only flowed on the earth—as the Indus, Vitastā, Asiknī, Paruṣṇī, Vipāṣ, Ṣutudrī, and Sarasvatī or Kubhā (Griffith 1963, Vol. I, p. 44n12)—but also were frequently regarded as divine or celestial (e.g. RV 1.164.3, 7.49.1–4, 7.103.2, 10.75.1ff).

There are also the seven rays of the Sun (RV 1.164.2–3), which are identified by the fourteenth-century authority Sāyaṇa with the seven sisters (RV 1.164.3 with n3). Another hymn (RV 1.50) referring to the seven solar rays seems to identify the Sun, Sūrya, in his fiery aspect, with Agni ('Knower of Creatures') (esp. verse 1) (as noted by O'Flaherty 1981, p. 189). This seems to link Sūrya's seven rays with Agni's seven rays or tongues. This hymn also refers to the seven solar rays as banners (verses 1 and 3), seven mares (verse 8), and 'the seven splendid daughters of the chariot' (verse 9; tr. O'Flaherty 1981). Incidentally, this hymn, again as noted by O'Flaherty (ibid.), appears to identify the Sun with Varuṇa (the eye of the gods) through the recurrent theme of seeing and being seen as well as giving light that enables others to see.

It may be that most, if not all, of these female heptads were regarded as varying manifestations of one and the same female heptad. It is true that some scholars reject the inclusion of certain heptads in such an equation; for instance, Tiwari cautions against equating the Seven Mothers of Agni with his seven flames, tongues, or rays (1985, p. 145). Yet, we must take account of the fact that Agni's seven sisters—who are identified with the Seven Mothers, as seen above—are described as 'red' (RV 10.5.5). In addition, Sāyaṇa's views, which support the equation of these sisters with Agni's seven tongues or flames (RV 10.5.5n5), ought to be taken at least as seriously as Tiwari's views. Further, the ability of the Seven Mothers to take various forms is indicated by a Ṛgvedic passage that describes them as having 'a hundred forms' (RG 10.97.2; O'Flaherty 1981, p. 285).

To understand these female heptads more deeply, let us now consider what roles these heptads were believed to play in relation to mankind. First of all, from what we have noted above, we see that the Seven Mothers gave birth to Agni and Soma, both of whom are Vedic deities of major importance. Also given birth by the Seven Mothers were, we might say, Sūrya and Varuṇa since, as we have seen above, the Sun seems to be identified with Agni and with Varuṇa (RV 1.50). Interestingly, Sūrya is described as being carried in a chariot by seven bay mares (RV 1.50.8).

The Seven Mothers, identified with the Seven Rivers, streams, or waters, are also said to 'send forth the hymn and prayer for gain of riches ... [and] for need of sacrifice disclose the udder' (RV 10.30.10–11). They 'send forth the rapture-giving wave ... which Indra drinks ... [and] the well that springeth from the clouds' (RV 10.30.9). The 'wave' is also referred to as their 'offspring and a well of sweetness' (RV 10.30.7–8). The waters are further portrayed as giving men life and birth, bringing men the life force, and helping men to find nourishment so that they can look upon great joy (RV 10.9.1–3). Thus, the Seven Mothers/Rivers/waters, etc., are the mothers of mankind and of all animate life and of the gods like Agni and Soma. Kramrisch, too, says that 'what all these heptads have in common is their maternity and their movement' (1975, p. 262). But these heptads are not just life- or birth-givers. They seem to give almost anything. For instance, they are described as giving men a horse, a cow, and a robe (RV 10.97.4), health and well-being (RV 10.9.4), cures (RV 10.9.5–7), medicines (RV 1.23.20–21; 10.97), healing balm (RV 1.23.19), sin-removing powers (RV 1.23.22; 10.9.8), thirst-quencher for cattle (RV 1.23.18), and so forth. The Seven Mothers/Rivers/waters would, thus, appear to be capable of giving almost anything auspicious and to fulfill innumerable roles. The only roles they do not play would seem to be inauspicious ones.

Having presented a brief general description of the early Vedic female heptads, I turn now to later Vedic literature and look, especially, at the Kṛttikās, the most important female heptad of this period for our purposes.

The Kṛttikās are a prominent constellation appearing, for the first time, in the texts of the later Vedic period (MacDonell & Keith

1967, pp. 411–15). Though, in classical Sanskrit literature, this constellation is usually regarded as six in number (Monier-Williams 1899, p. 304) or six plus one (this one being Arundhatī), there are earlier traditions counting seven stars in this constellation (MacDonell & Keith 1967, p. 415). A list of seven stars given in TS (4.4.5.b) goes: Ambā, Dulā, Nitatnī, Abhrayantī, Meghayantī, Varṣayantī, and Cupuṇīkā. These names are also found in the *Taittirīya Brāhmaṇa* and the *Kāṭhaka Saṃhitā* (MacDonell & Keith 1967, pp. 413–14). The importance given to the Kṛttikās in later Vedic literature is indicated by the prominent place occupied by this constellation in the rite of the consecration of sacred fire (*agnyādhāna*), as referred to in, e.g., the SB (2.1.2.1–5), the *Kāṭhaka Saṃhitā*, *Maitrāyaṇī Saṃhitā,* and the *Taittirīya Brāhmaṇa* (MacDonell & Keith 1967, p. 412). The Kṛttikās' importance is also shown by the fact that all the lists of the *nakṣatras* are headed by this constellation (ibid., p. 421).

A few examples of later Vedic references to the Kṛttikās may be given. The TS, at 4.4.10, contains the mantras for the *nakṣatra* bricks, arranged in a circle and beginning with the Kṛttikās. Here the Kṛttikās are associated with, among other gods, Agni especially. Another mantra for this constellation, found at TS 4.4.5.b, names the seven bricks (or stars), as has been noted above. There is a comment on this mantra in the same text at 5.3.9.

There is some more information on the nature of this constellation in other references. For instance, the afore-mentioned description given in the SB (2.1.2.1–5) of the basic *śrauta* rite of the *agnyādhāna* states reasons why one may set up the two principal fires under the Kṛttikās. The reasons include: that this constellation is 'doubtless Agni's asterism' (ibid., verse 1); that whereas the other lunar asterisms (*nakṣatras*) consist of 'one, two, three or four (stars)', the Kṛttikās have seven, and hence 'the most numerous' (ibid., verse 2); and that 'they [the Kṛttikās] do not move away from the eastern quarter, whilst the other asterisms do move from the eastern quarter' (ibid., verse 3). The next three verses, on the other hand, explain why it is also argued that one should not set up the fires under the Kṛttikās. The reason is that, though the Kṛttikās were the wives of the seven *ṛṣis* (or the Bears, Ursa Major), they were 'precluded from intercourse (with their husbands), for the latter, the seven rishis, rise in the north, and they (the Kṛttikās) in the east. Now it is a misfortune for one to be precluded from intercourse' (ibid., verse 4). Thus, by setting up the fires under the Kṛttikās, one might, thereby, be precluded from intercourse. The following verse, however, refutes the above argument by saying that one 'may nevertheless set up (his fire under the Kṛttikās); for Agni doubtless is their mate, and it is with Agni that they have intercourse: for this reason he may set up (the fire under the Kṛttikās)' (ibid., verse 5).

Two things that especially attract our attention in the above description of the Kṛttikās are, first, the great importance of this constellation in later Vedic literature and, second, the close association of the Kṛttikās with Agni, the Fire.

## 2.2 THE FEMALES' RELATIONSHIP WITH MALES

In the preceding section, I have briefly described some of the important female heptads of the early Vedic period as well as the Kṛttikās, who are a prominent constellation in later Vedic literature and who are, for our purposes, the most important female heptad of the later Vedic period.

When we focus our attention on the relationship between

females (who appear as heptads) and males, we find that two main patterns of male-female relationship are discernible in the Vedas. The first, which is probably the more prominent, is exemplified by the relationship of the Seven Mothers to Agni and to Soma. As we have seen, the seven females are the mothers of the male (Agni or Soma)—that is, they gave birth to him—and taught him for glory or in such things as ways of wisdom. In addition, they augment him. The Seven Mothers are where Agni's home is. In this pattern of the male-female relationship, the females are the mothers, and the male the child/baby. Though the male, when fully mature, is glorious and powerful, he certainly needs to be given instructions and protection, as well as birth, by his mothers. Further, the females' wisdom, which they impart to the male (child), and their power to give birth and to protect the male (child) are acknowledged by males themselves, who do not possess these qualities. For instance, the great fire-god Agni is portrayed as seeking, and being received by, 'heaven's Mighty Ones', also called 'Seven sounding Rivers' (RV 3.1.6), who are, as we have seen, equated with the Seven Mothers. As far as the females' power is concerned, it is not restricted to giving birth and providing protection alone, but seems to be almost unlimited, for the Seven Mothers are described as capable of giving almost anything auspicious, as we have seen above.

The second pattern, which is not recognizable until the later Vedic period, presents the females as the wives of the male(s). For instance, the waters are said to be 'the wives of Varuṇa' (TS 5.5.4.1). The Kṛttikās, on the other hand, are described as the wives of the seven *ṛṣis*, or the Great Bear (SB 2.1.2.4), as we have seen above. However, the marital relationship of these heptads is not quite straightforward, for the females seem, at the same time, to have an illicit relationship with Agni. The waters (the wives of Varuṇa), for instance, appear to be seduced by Agni. We read: 'Agni longed for them, he had union with them; his seed fell away, it became this (earth) ...' (TS5.5.4.1). The Kṛttikās, for their part, are precluded from intercourse with their husband and, instead, have intercourse with Agni (SB 2.1.2.4–5), as we have seen. The text does not say whether the Kṛttikās were separated from their husbands on account of their unfaithfulness to their husbands, or whether their separation preceded their relationship with Agni. Later myth writers mostly seem to have believed that the former was the case.

Let me, then, summarize this section as follows. In the early Vedic period, the females were the *mothers* of the male child (Agni/ Soma). In the later Vedic period, however, the females were *wives* of male(s) (Varuṇa or the seven *ṛṣis*); in the same period, they were either seduced by Agni or precluded from having intercourse with their own husbands, perhaps because of their unfaithfulness in having a relationship with Agni.

Do we notice a change in the nature of the male-female relationship over the two broad (early and later Vedic) periods? Perhaps, yes. But to speak of such a change in accurate terms, we really should find out whether there were any connections between the female heptads of the early and later Vedic periods. This is a complicated issue, and I shall discuss it in section 2.4 below. But for the sake of summarizing the present section, let me note that (as we shall see below) though there is no evidence to show that the seven mothers were regarded by the early Vedic composers as the Kṛttikās, some *later* Vedic composers seem to have believed that the later Vedic female heptads were linked with those of the early Vedic period. To give one example, we have, indeed, noted that the TS refers to the wives of Varuṇa as 'the waters' (4.5.4.1). If the later Vedic female heptads were thus regarded as connected with those of early Vedic literature, we might justifiably say that, as we move from the early to later Vedic periods, we witness the relegation of the female heptads from the position of domination and power in relation to males—viz. that of the mother—to the dominated and powerless position (in the context of the official Vedic culture), viz. that of wives. One interesting thing, however, is that something of the females' power still remained in the form of daring to have an illicit relationship with Agni.

## 2.3 MODE AND AIM OF WORSHIP/OTHER PRACTICE

Information that we have concerning the mode and aim of worship of the mothers in the early Vedic period indicates patterns of simple petitioning for their help. A good example is the RV hymn 7.49, which is addressed to the waters, also referred to as the goddesses. They are further identified with the Seven Rivers in verse 1. This hymn (tr. O'Flaherty 1981, p. 232) describes various features of the Seven Rivers—such as that they are 'waters of the sky' (verse 2) and 'pure and clear' (verses 2, 3), that they drip honey (verse 3), and that 'all the gods drink in ecstasy the exhilarating nourishment' among the waters (verse 4)—and each verse ends with the petition 'let the waters, who are goddesses, help me here and now'.

Hymn 10.9 from the RV also contains a petition to the waters. In this hymn, men ask for a variety of things, such as delicious sap, birth, the life force, cures, health, and drinking water. The Mothers' healing power is invoked in another hymn (RV 10.97), in which a doctor praises the healing plants that provide his medicines and prays that his patient be freed from disease. The Mothers, who are described as having numerous forms (verse 2), are here taking the form of the healing herbs. The Mothers are also said to have a thousand powers (ibid.).

Turning to the Kṛttikās, who are our most important heptad in late Vedic literature, we see that they are involved in the aforementioned rite of agnyādhāna (SB 2.1.2.1–5; described in detail in Kane, Vol. II, Part II, pp. 986ff). Upon completion of this rite, the sacrificer is said to attain the position of *āhitāgni* ('one who has consecrated the sacred Vedic fires' (Kane, ibid., p. 987)). This rite consists in 'the placing of burning coals for the generation of the gārhapatya and other fires at a particular time and place by a particular person to the accompaniment of certain mantras' (ibid.). Especially worth noting for us is the significance attached to the right season for a particular sacrificer and the right direction to be associated with a particular action. For instance, this rite may be performed, according to some sources, only 'on one of the seven nakṣatras, viz. Kṛttikā, Rohiṇī, Mṛgaśīrṣa, Pūrvā Phalgunī, Uttarā Phalgunī, Viśākhā, Uttarā Bhādrapadā (ibid., p. 986). Again, some sources specify a particular day in a particular season for a particular caste: e.g. on a *parva* day in spring for a brāhmaṇa (ibid., p. 987). Even in choosing the season, the sacrificer 'must have regard to the seven [above-mentioned] nakṣatras …' (ibid.).

Concerning the importance of a particular direction, it may be mentioned that the sacrificer requires a raised place for worship that slopes towards the east (ibid., pp. 988–89). The importance of the direction east is also emphasized in the SB (2.1.2.3), which, as we have seen above, says that one of the reasons for setting up the fires under the Kṛttikās is that this constellation does not move away from the eastern quarter. Further, the *nakṣatra* bricks, which are to be arranged in a circle, must begin with the Kṛttikās on the southeast (Keith 1914, p. 349n1).

I have looked at some of the important features of the worship that involves the female heptads of the Vedas. We shall have occasion to discuss the importance of the east in relation to the Kṛttikās again in the next section.

## 2.4 MEANING OF MULTIPLICITY

To discuss this topic in the context of this study, we need an idea of what connections might have existed between the Vedic female heptads and the later Saptamātṛkās, since we are looking at these Vedic heptads as a possible contributing factor in the formulation of the Saptamātṛkās. I begin by considering two most important suggestions so far made regarding the Vedic contribution to the formation of the concept of the Saptamātṛkās: one by Tiwari (1985) and the other by Harper (1977). As a preliminary note, it may be mentioned that Harper looks on all Vedic female heptads as having the Pleiades as their source (1977, pp. 30, 42), whereas Tiwari considers the Kṛttikās (appearing in later Vedic literature) as separate from the Seven Mothers of Agni and Soma, the Seven Rivers, etc. (who appear already in early Vedic literature) (1985, pp. 144–51).

Let me begin by looking at Tiwari's suggestion. First, regarding such female heptads of the early Vedic texts as Agni's Seven Mothers, Seven Sisters, seven tongues or rays, and Soma's Seven Mothers, Tiwari rejects the idea—which has been suggested by some scholars—that these heptads can be considered the prototype of the Saptamātṛkās. Among Tiwari's reasons for this rejection, the following two concern us especially. (1) The Mothers of Agni or Soma, etc., betray 'nothing of the character of the Mātṛs as reflected in classical Sanskrit literature' (1985, p. 145) such as the Mbh, in which, as Tiwari says, the mothers 'appear essentially as groups of unbrahmanical, anonymous deities of indefinite number and mainly demoniacal nature' (ibid., p. 146). (2) The essential nature of the Saptamātṛkās of the Purāṇas—viz. that they are the personified energies of seven male deities—is not anticipated in Vedic literature (ibid.).

In regard to Tiwari's reason (1), it is true that early Vedic descriptions of the Seven Mothers of Angi or Soma, the Seven Sisters, the Seven Rivers, etc. do not suggest any demoniacal nature. However, we may mention three things briefly. It may be significant that a passage from the *Muṇḍaka Upaniṣad* (though this text does not belong to the period we are concerned with) mentions the names of Agni's 'Seven red Sisters' anonymously referred to in the RV 10.5.5. The passage reads:

> Kālī (black), Karālī (terrific), Manojavā (swift as thought), Sulohitā (very red), Sudhūmravarṇa (purple), Sphuliṅginī (sparkling), and the brilliant Viṣvarūpī (having all forms), all these playing about are called the seven tongues (of fire) (1.2.4; Müller 1965, p. 31).

The names Kālī and Karālī, which connote death association, suggest that this female heptad may have possessed chthonic or demoniacal significance. We may also note in passing that Kālī, as Harper (1977, p. 30) says, is very similar to Cāmuṇḍā of the Saptamātṛkās. Further, these two are 'not distinguished conceptually or iconographically' in the Kathmandu Valley (Slusser 1982, p. 330).

Another thing worth noting is that the 'waters' are given a tinge of inauspiciousness in a TS passage that we have mentioned above. Though the TS is a later text than the period we are considering here, it is interesting to note that this passage portrays the waters—who are here the wives of Varuṇa—as succumbing to Agni's seduction. In the orthodox Brahmanical context, this would definitely suggest *adharma*.

One more thing may be said regarding Tiwari's reason (1). It is true that large numbers of Mātṛs in classical Sanskrit literature are demoniacal, and that early Vedic references to the Seven Mothers of Angi, etc., do not suggest such a character. Yet, it is also true that at least one group of females in classical Sanskrit literature—significantly, the six wives of the sages—is free of any demoniacal character (though they are less chaste than Arundhatī, perhaps).

I now turn to Tiwari's reason (2). Tiwari says that the central feature of the fully-developed Saptamātṛkās of the Purāṇas—viz. that the seven females are male deities' personified energies—is not found in the early Vedic groups of seven females. It is true. This feature, however, is hardly recognizable in classical Sanskrit literature, either. The possible exceptions are, perhaps, the wives of the seven sages and the *Śalya Parva*'s portrayal (ch. 46; Ganjuli 1981, p. 129) of some of the mothers as partaking of the nature of Yama, some of Rudra, some of Soma, some of Kuvera, and so forth. In either case, however, the females are not described as personified energies of the males.

Tiwari's views that we are now considering, in fact, form a part of his argument that—despite several scholars' attempts to find the prototype of the Saptamātṛkās in early Vedic literature—one cannot refer to any of the female heptads of early Vedic literature as the prototype of the Saptamātṛkās (1985, pp. 144–49). Though I disagree with some of the things he says, I do believe that it is difficult, if not impossible, to identify *the* 'prototype' of the Saptamātṛkās in early Vedic literature, or in any other single tradition for that matter. This is because all the traditions, as they are known to us now, probably contain adaptations from elsewhere. While it would be useful if the prototype of the Saptamātṛkās could be positively identified, this identification would appear to be extremely difficult. Nevertheless, this difficulty should not deter us from investigating the early Vedic female heptads carefully. Our aim is to examine the significance of multiplicity as associated with the Saptamātṛkās. Thus, to gain as accurate an understanding as possible, we are looking at every possible source that might have contributed to the formation of the Saptamātṛkās. Since we are interested in 'multiplicity' as manifested in the Saptamātṛkās, it is natural for us to be concerned with any female grouping of the right number—that is, seven. From this approach, however, it does not need to follow that we regard any of these groups as *the* 'prototype' of the Saptamātṛkās, as such. Indeed, if a number of different sources contributed to the formation of the Saptamātṛkās (as the case might be), then postulating a single 'prototype' may not be wise at all.

We have examined Tiwari's sceptical views on the connection between the early Vedic female heptads and the Saptamātṛkās. In turning, next, to Tiwari's suggestion concerning the Kṛttikās' relation to the Saptamātṛkās, we move to later Vedic literature. What he says here is that one cannot derive the later Mātṛs from the Kṛttikās, partly because one cannot prove the existence of a popular cult centring on this constellation (1985, p. 151). Another reason is that the Skanda-myths in the Mbh, in which the fully developed Mātṛs of later Hinduism are recognizable for the first time, 'do not warrant the derivation of the "Mothers" from a specific group like the Kṛttikās' (ibid.), for many of the Mātṛs in this text are, as we have noted, essentially groups of demoniacal nature and of indefinite number (ibid., pp. 145–46).

To this argument, however, one might object that several elements (apart from the number seven) of the Mātṛs cult and belief seem to be anticipated in later Vedic descriptions of the Kṛttikās. First, the Kṛttikās are described as wives of the seven *ṛṣis* in the BS (2.1.2.4) already. Second, that text seems to suggest the Kṛttikās' somewhat inauspicious or dangerous nature, viz. their illicit relationship with Agni. This might be connected with the demoniacal character of the later Mātṛs. Third, this association of the seven sages' wives (i.e. Kṛttikās) with Agni foreshadows the Mbh account (3.213.40ff) of Skanda's birth. Incidentally, another later Vedic story that anticipates this Skanda-myth is the TS account of Varuṇa's wives called the waters, who have an illicit intercourse with Agni (5.5.4.1; considered above). Fourth, though Tiwari says that 'the Skanda myth in the Mbh does not clearly allude to the astral nature of the wives of the seers' (1985, p. 153), this text does, in fact, hint at such a nature, for these wives are described there as 'radiant like golden altars, spotless like a digit of the moon, glowing with the glow of fire, all marvellous like stars' (Mbh 3.213.43f; tr. van Buitenen 1975, p. 649).

All in all, it would appear that, despite Tiwari's sceptical views on the connection between the Vedic female heptads and the Saptamātṛkās, it makes sense for us to look to Vedic female heptads for possible contributions to the formulation of the symbolical meaning of female multiplicity as found in the Saptamātṛkās.

Harper (1977, pp. 21–45) does precisely that. Therefore, mainly drawing on her material, I shall summarize some of the Vedic meanings of feminine multiplicity that seem relevant to the Saptamātṛkās. I begin by noting that the importance of the number seven in the Vedas is well known (e.g. Hastings' *Encyclopaedia of Religion and Ethics*, Vol. 9, pp. 407ff; Keith 1971, pp. 41, 79, 103, 105, etc.; Monier-Williams 1899, p. 1147). An impressive list of the Vedic heptads, both male and female, representing a variety of different aspects of life, is given by Harper (1977, pp. 28ff), such as seven wild and domestic animals, the seven plants, the seven senses and life breaths, the seven regions of the universe, the seven suns, seven priests singing prayers composed of seven metres or seven syllables, the seven notes of the harp, the seven layers of bricks in the altars, and so on. Indeed, the Vedic scriptures employ heptads so frequently that it is only fair to suppose that the number seven and multitudes of seven had intrinsic significance to the Vedic Aryans.

Harper suggests that the main reason for imparting great value to the number seven was that certain important natural phenomena were presented in septpartite groupings (1977, pp. 33–37), and that these exerted profound influence on the structuring of the Vedic thought. Some examples may be given. First, the visible 'planets' of the solar system were seven in number, Saturn, Venus, Jupitar, Mercury, Mars, Moon, and Sun (ibid., p. 33). The seven worlds described in the Vedas possibly represented these planets (ibid.). Second, the diatonic musical scale has seven tones, which must have been connected with the seven tones of the priests and *ṛṣis*, the seven voices or tones of Vāk, the goddess of speech, and the seven notes of the harp (ibid., p. 34). Third, there were also the seven colours of the visible spectrum—red, orange, yellow, green, blue, indigo, and violet (ibid.)—which may have been represented by the seven bay mares of Sūrya, the Sun (ibid., p. 35). Fourth, the lunar cycle is a multiple heptad, there being twenty-eight days to a cycle (ibid., p. 35). Fifth, also totalling twenty-eight were the *nakṣatras* (lunar mansions) that correspond to the twenty-eight lunar days; the moon travels through these constellations in the course of its lunar cycle (ibid., p. 36; for the *nakṣatras*, see also MacDonell & Keith 1968, pp. 409ff). The number of the *nakṣatras* is also stated as twenty-seven, but, as MadDonell & Keith (ibid., p. 411) say, 'it is perfectly possible that 28 is the earlier number, and that Abhijit dropped out because it was faint, or too far north....' Sixth, all the lists of the *nakṣatras* invariably begin with the Kṛttikās, which as we have seen were composed of seven stars (TS 4.4.5.b, etc.). And seventh, there were other constellations consisting of seven stars, such as the Ursa Major (the seven *ṛṣis*). Thus, says Harper, the septpartite nature of certain natural phenomena significant to the ancient man must have been applied to various aspects of his life so as to

> arrange the entire world scheme and patterns of living on the basis of seven in order to participate or exist in harmony with the cosmic rhythm (1977, pp. 36–37).

What is signified by the number seven in the above instances may be the completion of a cycle and the beginning of a new cycle. The totality of the seven planets, each symbolizing a different sphere of existence, probably represented the wholeness of the universe, which might be regarded as a higher order than the seven individual spheres. In music, a new cycle begins when one moves on to the eighth note, which is again the first note. The seven colours of the visible spectrum together completes one set of prismatic colours. The twenty-eight lunar days—a multiple of seven—evidently bring the completion, or end, or death and rebirth, of the lunar cycle over and over. The moon is likely to have been used to calculate time because of its conspicuous periodicities (Harper 1977, p. 35, citing Eliade). Linked with the lunar cycle is the first of the *nakṣatras*, the Pleiades (Kṛttikās), the rising of which, as we saw earlier, marked the beginning of the yearly time cycle and, moreover, of the agricultural year. We have some indications that, to the Vedic Aryans too, the Pleiades signified the beginning of a new year or cycle. In the building of the Vedic fire altar—which Eliade says marked the remaking of the world, of the year, and of time (1954, p. 80)—it is the Kṛttikās brick that was the first to be placed of all the twenty-eight *nakṣatra* bricks that formed a circular fire ring, according to the TS (4.4.10; noted by Harper 1977, p. 41). It is likely that the seven divine stars of the Kṛttikās, represented by the brick, were regarded as marking the completion and re-creation of yet another yearly cycle. The seven, then, probably symbolized a cyclic (e.g. yearly) renewal.

Incidentally, in response to the suspicion that the Vedic astronomers were not accurate observers (MacDonell & Keith 1967, p. 423), we may note in passing that evidence does suggest that the Vedic Aryans' astronomical knowledge was fairly advanced (Kane 1974, Vol. V, Part I, pp. 477ff, 488ff, etc.), the moon and stars in general playing a significant role in the Vedic life and thought (ibid., pp. 506–07, 523ff). Even Tiwari believes that astro cults in the Vedic period were of such significance that they could have influenced the later cult of the Mātṛs (1985, pp. 151–55).

Returning to the Kṛttikās, Harper further sees this constellation as connected with the earlier Vedic female heptads such as the Seven Mothers of Agni and of Soma, for 'as the "introducers of the year", the ones who give birth, they are the great primordial mothers on whom all that follows depends' (ibid., p. 42). Though the obvious objection that this would be reading later meaning into the RV is perfectly possible, there is an indication that this constellation may have received considerable attention from the Aryans much earlier than the later Vedic period, from which all our explicit literary references to the Kṛttikās date. The SB (2.1.2.3; noted above) says that the Kṛttikās 'do not move away from the eastern quarter, whilst the other asterisms do move from the eastern quarter' (tr. Eggeling 1882, p. 282). As stressed by Kane (1974, Vol. V, Part I, p. 507n733), the present tense is employed in this sentence, an indication that this passage represents a tradition that existed when the Kṛttikās' position on the equator was an observed fact. The eastern horizon, from which stars and the sun rise, must have attracted the ancient star observers, and the due east is defined by the sunrise at the vernal equinox, to which the Pleiades corresponded around 2240 BCE (e.g. Parpola 1985, p. 100). There are also some Vedic references to the spring as 'head of the year', etc., which confirm that, in the tradition recorded in such texts, the year started at the vernal equinox (ibid.). This might reinforce the significance of the Kṛttikās as an indicator of the beginning of the year and a symbol of yearly cyclic renewal. Thus, it is not improbable that the Pleiades was significant to the Ṛgvedic composers as well.

There are also some other indications of the connection between the Kṛttikās and the Ṛgvedic Seven rivers, Seven Mothers of Agni and of Soma, etc. For instance, as pointed out by Harper (1977, p. 43), the mantra for the Kṛttikās in the TS 4.4.10 refers to these seven stars as 'the radiances of Agni ... [and] of Soma' (tr. Keith 1914, p. 349). This association of the Kṛttikās with both Agni and Soma suggests a connection between this constellation and the Seven Mothers. Some other indications connect the Kṛttikās with the waters/the Seven Rivers (identified with the Seven Mothers, as seen above). The names of the seven stars include three that are clearly linked with water or rainfall: Abhrayantī (forming clouds), Meghayantī (making cloudy), and Varṣayantī (causing rain) (MacDonell & Keith 1967, p. 415). A fourth name, Dulā, may derive from the Semitic Hebrew root *dili* (a pot for pouring water) (Harper 1977, p. 45). Further, the seven mother streams of the RV later became Varuṇa's wives and, as we have noted, got involved in the kind of relationship with Agni that suggests a connection with the Kṛttikās. It is not impossible, therefore, that the seven Rivers/Mothers, etc., were connected with the Kṛttikās, though no explicit reference exists to prove it.

I now summarize this discussion. Though the real meaning of the number seven may be irretrievably lost in the distant past, we might say, on the basis of the foregoing, that the number seven was a number of great significance and power in that it symbolizes the completion (or end) and re-creation of various cycles that were important to the Vedic people—e.g., cycles that relate to the levels of music, time calculation, the septpartite cosmological structure, etc. Perhaps we might say that it was a number essential to the rhythmic patterns of the Vedic cosmos, and that its significance lied in its power of cyclic renewal, which enabled men to return to an original point, a new beginning of another cycle.

We have looked at a number of female heptads appearing in Vedic literature, including the Seven Rivers and the Seven Mothers of Agni and Soma from the earlier Vedic period and the Kṛttikās from the later Vedic period. Particularly noteworthy were the Kṛttikās, which were regarded as a symbol of the completion and beginning of the yearly time cycle.

The power of the number seven has been expressed by Harper as: 'To reach or surpass seven is to be born again into a higher order' (1977, p. 47). Related to this intrinsic power of seven, it seems, is the power of the Seven Mothers, etc., of the earlier Vedic period to give men almost anything auspicious (e.g. the life force, fire, Soma, health, etc.) and the power of Kṛttikās to renew or regenerate the year or to effect yearly renewal, a yearly return to the original beginning.

# 3. ABORIGINAL/DRAVIDIAN SEVEN SISTERS/VIRGINS

## 3.1 GENERAL DESCRIPTION

Before proceeding to consider the Saptamātṛkās themselves (in chapter 4), I look in chapter 3 at the Dravidian or aboriginal[2] Seven Sisters or Virgins. At the outset, it may be mentioned that, though most of the material that I draw on comes from relatively recent times, there are indications that the Dravidian culture may have been of considerable antiquity. For instance, Dravidian languages seem to have been prevalent during the second millennium BCE in North India, as indicated by the fact that the RV uses words that were borrowed from the Dravidians (Harper 1977, p. 15). At any rate, whatever the nature of interaction (if any) between the Dravidians and the Aryans may have been, one interesting fact for us is that both peoples seem to have possessed the mother cult of groups of seven females.

It would appear that many groups of Seven Sisters/Virgins are specifically associated with disease, though sometimes such specific association does not occur. I shall first look at some examples of Seven Sisters that have no specific disease association. In Masulipatam on the east coast of Andhra Pradesh, the local fishermen worship the following group of seven (one of them is associated with disease): Mutyalamma (the Pearl Goddess), Chinnintamma (the Goddess who is the head of the house), Challalamma (Goddess who presides over buttermilk), Ghantalamma (Goddess who goes with bells), Yamparamma (Goddess who transacts business), Mamilamma (Goddess who sits under the mango tree), and Gangamma

[2] For the usage of these terms, I follow Harper (1977, p. 47).

(Goddess who protects against smallpox) (Whitehead 1921, p. 23). Each goddess is said to be of a very gentle nature and help the fishermen in their daily life.

The Seven Virgins (Kannimar) are favoured by a forest tribe called Eravallar in Cochin State. Good goddesses, the Kannimar look after the well-being of the family (Harper 1977, p. 66). Such groups of Seven Virgins seem popular especially in the southernmost part of India (ibid., pp. 65–66).

In the Tamil country, Mariamma, who is worshipped in almost every village (Whitehead 1921, pp. 31–32), is the goddess of smallpox—she is the Tamil equivalent of Śītalā of North India. Unlike Śītalā, however, Mariamma is not connected with the Seven Sisters/ Virgins; Mariamma keeps aloof from the Seven Sisters and is never found in any temples that are dedicated to the latter (ibid. p. 32). The Seven Sisters, unlike Mariamma, are described as gentle (ibid.) and their main concern is with protecting the well-being of the villagers by warding off evils, looking after the fertility of cattle and goats, and giving children (Harper 1977, p. 66).

In Mysore State, too, groups of Seven Sisters who are not specifically connected with disease and who are benign are worshipped, each village having its own set of names for them (Whitehead 1921, p. 29). In Mysore City and its environs, the sevens' names are 'Bisal Mari (connected with the sun), Goonal Mari, Kel Mari (earthen pot), Yeeranagere Mari, Hiridevathi (eldest sister), Chammandamma and Uttahnahaliamma' (ibid., p. 80).

Maharashtra retains an old tradition in which we now have *sati-apsara* 'the seven Apsaras (celestial nymphs)' (Kosambi 1962, p. 86). They are essentially water spirits promoting fertility (Harper 1977, p. 58–59). Another group of Seven Sisters associated with water are described in a myth possessed by an Orissan tribe called Gadaba. The seven are maidens of water or the seven streams/oceans brought forth from the saliva of Indra for the purpose of extinguishing Fire, who was ravishing the world (Harper 1977, p. 59).

Not all groups of Seven Sisters that have no specific association with disease are benign and gentle. Many have a chthonic nature, and often ambivalent characteristics are evident. A good example is given by Whitehead:

> Saptakannigais (the seven virgins), or Akasakannigais (the heavenly virgins), are the tutelary deities of tanks, and the figures of the Kannigais seated in a row are often carved on a small stone and placed on tank bunds, especially at places where the tank has been breached. In the North Arcot district they are described as female creatures who are very quarrelsome, and, when they fight, breaches are caused in the tanks by the stamping of their feet. At the same time they are supposed to protect tanks, and when the flood rises to a dangerous point, it is said that one of the Kannigais, in the shape of a little child, runs through the village knocking at the doors and calling up the villagers to come and protect the bund. It is believed that people walking alone along a tank bund have sometimes met the Saptakannigais, going in procession with horses and torches, and that anyone who sees them invariably dies (1921, p. 26).

Let us look next at the Seven Sisters/Virgins that are specifically connected with disease. Here, ambivalence is one of their essential features, since the goddesses seem both to inflict disease and to restore health. Some examples of this type of Seven Sisters follow. One shrine on the outskirts of Bangalore is dedicated to Annamma (the presiding goddess), Chandeśvaramma, Māyeśvaramma, Maramma (the goddess of cholera), Udalamma (goddess of swollen necks), Kokkalamma (goddess of coughs), and Sukhajamma (goddess of smallpox and measles) (ibid., p. 29).

The Seven Sisters and their brother Pŏtu Rāza of Kandukuru Taluq, who have been described by Elmore, exemplify the village deities of the Telugu area (1913, pp. 12–26). The Sisters' names are Poleramma (the well-known goddess of smallpox), Ankamma (a household goddess represented by a pot), Muthyalamma, Dilli Polasi (both a village and household goddess), Bangaramma, Mathamma (the especial goddess of the Madigas), and Renuka. The most important and best known is Poleramma, whose shrine is usually outside the village and often on the bank of an irrigation tank or reservoir (ibid., p. 12). Though also responsible for all other troubles like cattle disease, drought, and the people's sickness in general, 'the name Poleramma ... is the common expression among the people for smallpox' (ibid., p. 13). When smallpox breaks out in a village, she is considered to be angry, the disease being an expression of her anger, and to have come to the people.

The goddess of smallpox is famous throughout India. In the North, she is commonly known as Śītalā, who is often considered one of the seven sisters by whom the pustular groups of diseases are thought to be inflicted (Crooke 1896, pp. 127–28). Crooke reports three main lists of seven names for Śītalā and her Sisters (ibid., pp. 128–29). One list goes: Śītalā, Masānī (the deity of the cremation ground), Basanti (the yellow goddess, probably related to the skin condition caused by the diseases concerned), Mahā Māī (the great Mother), Polamdě (she who makes the body soft or flabby), Lamkariyā (she that hastens), and Agwānī (the leader, but also has some association with smallpox). Another list, which comes from Hardwār, is: Śītalā, Sedalā, Runukī, Jhunukī, Mihilā, Merhalā, and Mandilā. A third list is given as: Śītalā, Phūlmatī, Chamariyā, Dhurgā Kālī, Mahā Kālī, and Bhadrā Kālī. These goddesses of the last group are connected with various forms of pustular disease. For instance, part of the name of Phūlmatī probably means the pustules (*phūl*) of the disease (ibid., p. 129). Her form of the disease is said to be the mildest, the worst being Śītalā's, while a very bad form of confluent smallpox is attributed to Chamariyā.

A group of Seven Sisters that is similar in nature to the last group is also reported by Babb (1975, pp. 129ff). His informants say that the expression 'Seven Sisters' refers to seven different varieties of smallpox, distinguished by particular types of skin eruption. These Seven Sisters may also be referred to by the one name Śītalā. Śītalā is feared 'particularly in the hot season when she moves about the countryside entering the villages, houses, and bodies of those with whom she is annoyed' (ibid., p. 129). Since a patient of smallpox is considered to be possessed by the goddess, the therapy consists in 'cooling' her anger to effect her withdrawal (ibid.). A folktale preserved in this tradition contains one of the widespread patterns of the origin of disease goddesses in folk culture: Unjust mistreatment, coupled with male aggression, produces disease goddesses (O'Flaherty 1980, p. 101, citing Brubaker 1978). This folktale connects the goddesses' anger (=cause of smallpox) with seven virgins who were abandoned by their father and who wandered about, hot and thirsty (Babb 1975, p. 131).

This pattern of disease goddess production is also found in the birth of the twenty-one (a multiple of seven) disease goddesses of the Baiga of Rewa State in the Central Provinces. A folktale tells us that

> a new bride named Piri Deshahi was enraged when her husband seduced one of her seven sisters on their wedding night. As a result of her anger, she gave birth to twenty-one daughters who were responsible for all the diseases which plague man and cattle (Harper 1977, pp. 59–60).

In the village of Shanti Nagar, a traditional ceremony known as Sili Sat (Cold Seventh) is held annually in the month of Chait (March–April) by women of the village in honour of Śītalā and her six sisters (Freed & Freed 1962, p. 262). One of the important features of the ceremony is food offerings made to the seven sisters, the purpose of which is said to be to protect children from disease and, in general, to ensure the welfare of children as well as the protection of calves and other animals that are important to the household (ibid., p. 263). These seven sisters are interpreted by the women as responsible for bringing illness to children as well as protecting children (ibid., p. 265). The women themselves can hardly name all the seven, but according to a Brahmin teacher of Sanskrit, their names and disease associations are: Chechak or Śitala Mata (smallpox), Khanti Mata (typhoid), Khelnimelni Mata (the sickness does not bother the child and he can go on playing), Khasra Mata (measles), Khamera Mata (tetanus), Phulki Mata (boils), Mursal Mata (mumps and big red boils) (ibid., p. 269).

It may be worth noting that, here and in other areas, diseases frequently represented by these Seven Sisters/Virgins affect children especially. Another thing we may note is that the seven goddesses are Virgins and yet sometimes also regarded as Mothers (Babb 1975, p. 226; Crooke 1896, p. 126).

Though the groups of Seven Sisters/Virgins presented above are only a small fraction of the rich and varied folk traditions involving village goddesses, they do indicate, despite varied characteristics of these groups, that the number seven is of great significance in the grouping of folk goddesses throughout much of India. I shall look at this theme in detail in section 3.4 below.

## 3.2 THE FEMALES' RELATIONSHIP WITH MALES

We shall briefly note two prominent facts regarding the females' relationship with males in aboriginal/Dravidian worship of Seven Sisters/Virgins. The first is the afore-mentioned motif of male aggression and unjust mistreatment suffered by females (which frequently leads to the production of disease goddesses). This motif (if it does not always produce disease goddesses) is recurrent in folklore's explanations of the goddesses' *anger* (often requiring the sacrifice of a male(s), human or animal, to appease it) or some form of manifestation of the goddesses' *power*.

As an example of the former, we may mention the story of a sage named Taṭikkāra Vīrappaṉ and the Seven Virgins associated with a tank, as reported by Hiltebeitel (1988, p. 59). When the sage went to the tank at a time inappropriate for a human and chanced to see the Seven Virgins bathing there, the latter were enraged. Their wrath, caused by the male violation of female chastity, eventually had him killed. On the other hand, an instance of the combination of male aggression and the unjust mistreatment of females resulting in a manifestation of feminine power is found, e.g., in an Orissan myth from the Juang tribe (Harper 1977, p. 59) in which seven sisters, after dancing for seven days, were chased by a mischievous brother. The myth says that their hair and ornaments that fell to the ground while they were on the run gave rise to sago and toddy palms, thus subsequently bringing toddy into the world. So, male aggression and injustice resulted in the manifestation of the feminine *power of intoxication*.

The second prominent fact to be noted in this section is the recurrent association, in South India, of the Seven Sisters/Virgins with Potu-rāja, who is described most frequently as the younger brother of the Seven Sisters (Hiltebeitel 1988, pp. 348–49). But the identity of this male figure is actually not very straightforward. He is also often a servant (Beck 1981, p. 122n63), or an attendant (Elmore 1913, p. 17) of the goddess. He is sometimes a husband of the goddess (Whitehead 1921, p. 18). His caste identity is not clear, either, for he is sometimes said to be a son of an outcast, and sometimes a Brahmin. He is also closely associated with the buffalo sacrifice, an association that may show his original identity as, not the goddesses' younger brother, but lover or husband. This is a complex issue, and it can only be outlined here (relation between Potu-rāja and the buffalo sacrifice has been dealt with by, especially, Hiltebeitel (1978), Beck (1981), and Onishi (1995)). The main clues to finding out his true identity include the following. First, his name, Potu-rāja, means 'buffalo-king'. Second, in the buffalo sacrifice, the official responsible for biting to death a sheep or goat—which is a secondary sacrificial animal, the main being a buffalo—is referred to by this name in Maharashtra and Karnataka (Hiltebeitel 1980, p. 190). Interestingly enough, this official, after the main part of the sacrifice is done, carries the buffalo's severed head on his own when leading those men who are going to a boundary location to scatter rice soaked in sacrificial animals' blood (ibid., p. 195). Further, after the buffalo's head is buried on the boundary line, all go home except the 'Potu-rāja', who must stay away and is not to be seen for three days (ibid.). This practice may confirm Potu-rāja's identity as a buffalo, or buffalo demon. His demonic origins are often suggested in folklore, too (Hiltebeitel 1988, p. 351, etc.). Third, the main animal to be sacrificed, viz. the buffalo, is usually identified as the husband of the village goddess (Hiltebeitel 1980, pp. 190–91). Fourth, the question of why the consort is to be killed may be answered by looking at folklore that indicates that an idea of castration very likely explains the practice of the buffalo sacrifice. For instance, the standard practice of cutting off the right foreleg of the buffalo and putting it in the animal's mouth may be accounted for by a myth of a girl/goddess who was deceived by a low-caste man disguised as a Brahmin into marrying him and who, upon discovering her lover's deceit, beheaded him, castrated him, and thrusted his severed penis into his own mouth (Beck 1981, p. 122n63). In the mythical context, a male being castrated by the women he tries to seduce is not an uncommon motif (O'Flaherty 1973, pp. 173–74, 177, 180–81, 183–84). Fifth, Maharashtra's buffalo-related figure, named Mhasoba (=Mahiṣāsura), is also understood as both the victim and consort of the goddess (Kosambi 1962, pp. 2–3, 85–91). Sixth, in Tamil literary sources, too, parallels to such a pattern have been shown to exist (Shulman 1980, pp. 175–211).

Though the above is only a few elements of this complex issue, I hope I have give enough material to demonstrate that the relationship between Potu-rāja and the Seven Sisters may well have involved the idea that male aggression and injustice suffered by females results in females' anger or in the manifestation of females' real power.[3]

## 3.3 MODE AND AIM OF WORSHIP/OTHER PRACTICE

Let us briefly note some examples of the worship of the Seven Sisters, representing various geographical areas and some of the essential features of the worship of the Seven Sisters/Virgins. We shall begin with North India. In the village of Shanti Nagar in Delhi State, a festival known as Sili Sat (Cold Seventh) is held in the month of Chait (March–April), as reported by Freed & Freed (1962). Traditionally, this marks the onslaught of the hot season in which children, especially, formerly had the most sickness of pustulating disease, such as smallpox. The main part of this ceremony is the offering of festive food to the goddesses and the pouring of water. The participants also cleaned a pond identified as the mother-queen's pond. The purpose of the food offerings, as we have noted above, is to ensure the protection and welfare of children and animals of importance to the household (ibid., p. 263). Only women took part in this ceremony, which is neglected by men.

In Muzaffarnagar District in Upper India, there is a shrine dedicated to Śītalā as Ujalī Mātā ('the White Mother'). Crooke reported that vast crowds had gathered there and that women had

[3] The currently widespread understanding of Potu-rāja as the Goddesses' younger brother is probably explained, as Beck (1981, p. 122n63) says, by the fact that the standard procedure of placing the buffalo's foreleg in its mouth is now merely seen as expressing the victim's submission to the goddess and as involving nothing sexual. The position of a 'younger brother' can be connected with the idea of submission and is desexualized compared with that of a 'lover'.

made vows for the boon of sons and, upon bestowal of it, fulfilled their vows through the necessary offerings to the goddess (1896, p. 127). Crooke interpreted the peculiar practice of releasing calves at this shrine as a survival of the rite of cattle sacrifice (ibid.).

In some places in the North-west Provinces, in which Śītalā is worshipped along with her six sisters, a very bad form of confluent smallpox is interpreted as the work of Chamariyā, one of the six sisters, who is then to be propitiated through the slaughtering of a pig by a Chamar or other low-caste priest (ibid., p. 129). Three of this set of six sisters are variant forms of Kālī, who are responsible for types of pustular diseases other than smallpox and require as propitiatory offerings 'cakes, sweetmeats, pigs, goats, sheep, and black fowls' (ibid.).

In the worship of the Seven Sisters reported by Babb (1975, pp. 129–35), symptoms of smallpox are understood as the goddesses' displeasure and a case of smallpox as an instance of possession. The patient, therefore, is regarded as possessing oracular powers, and Śītalā (all the seven sisters are often represented by her alone) may, through the patient's mouth, make requests—such as the sacrifice of a goat—which must be honoured for the recovery of the patient.

An instance of the worship of Śītalā in Bengal may also be looked at. She

> is worshipped on a piece of ground marked out and smeared with cow-dung. A fire being lighted, and butter and spirits thrown upon it, the worshipper makes obeisance, bowing his forehead to the ground and muttering incantations. A hog is then sacrificed, and the bones and

> offal being burnt, the flesh is roasted and eaten, but no one must take home with him any scrap of the victim (Crooke 1896, p. 126).

Turning to the South, we find that a fire-walking ceremony is an important part of an annual festival that is held in honour of the seven goddesses at a shrine on the outskirts of Bangalore. It is noteworthy that apart from the *pūjārī* who takes the lead in this ceremony, the fire-walking is done by women, who have lighted *āratīs* (oil lamps) on their heads (Whitehead 1921, pp. 79–80). Another instance of fire-walking is reported from Mysore City (ibid., p. 80) and many areas of Madras State (Harper 1977, p. 63).

The Seven Sisters of Mysore receive an annual festival lasting about four weeks, as reported by Whitehead (1921, pp. 80ff). Whitehead says that it is held generally in February, though according to Harper (1977, p. 62) it may be celebrated during the period from February to May, depending on the village. The festival often includes hook swinging. Animals are slaughtered, and rice is cooked and mixed with the animal's blood. The blood-soaked rice is sprinkled over the streets while a killed goat or sheep is dragged on the way. Upon the severed heads of sacrificial buffaloes lights are placed, the faces are smeared with fat, turmeric, and kunkuma. The right foreleg of each buffalo is cut off and placed into the mouth. Harper also says that *pūjārī* drinks some of the blood of the victims and eats some of their flesh in a state of possession (ibid.). Usually, after the main part of the ceremony is done, the head of the buffalo is taken to a boundary location and left at the border of the village lands (ibid., p. 63).

The Agasas in Mysore State believe that illness is caused by the Seven Sisters. Their pūjās, held when illness occurs, involve the setting up of seven stones in a small shed near a water course and the offering of sacrificial animals and fruit, coconuts, etc. (Harper 1977, p. 63).

In regard to the worship of the Seven Sisters of Kandukuru Taluq—which exemplifies the practices of the Telugu area—Elmore reports (1913, pp. 12–26) that a separate ceremony is offered for each of the seven, except for Renuka. In each case, the sister is represented by a clay pot(s). Animals, especially buffaloes, are slaughtered. The official responsible for this ritual is a Madiga (outcast). He also functions as the *asadi* (story teller). An oil lamp is placed on the severed head of the animal, and the blood is soaked into boiled rice, which is sprinkled at boundary locations of the village.

In the Tamil area, the worship of the Seven Virgins often uses seven bricks or stones placed in an enclosure under a margosa tree, in a small hut, or in a separate brick temple, but brass pots are also sometimes used to represent the seven goddesses. Usually the seven goddesses receive camphor or flowers as offerings but, on special occasion, coconuts, fowls, goats, or sheep, and pigs are offered (Whitehead 1921, pp. 94ff; Harper 1977, pp. 66–67). In the Trichinopoly district, after the sacrificial sheep is beheaded, a *pūjārī* sucks some of its blood in a state of possession (Whitehead 1921, p. 99). Then, four or five pigs are beheaded, their blood is offered to the goddesses, and later the blood is mixed with boiled rice to be scattered (ibid.).

By way of summary, I suggest that three main aims are discernible in the worship of the Seven Sisters: fertility, protection, and purgation. The three are not necessarily mutually exclusive, but the first two tend to be found in ceremonies held annually, and the latter in those held as occasion demands (e.g. when an epidemic breaks out). First, regarding fertility, many village ceremonies seem to be aimed at ensuring the propagation of crops, herds, and human offspring. If these specific purposes are not explicit, the association with fertility is implicit in, for example, the way the sacrificial animal's blood—whose great beneficial power is indicated by particular ceremonial procedures (Hiltebeitel 1980, p. 191)—is treated. We have seen that the blood is sometimes offered to the goddess, and that blood-soaked rice is often scattered on the ground. The blood may also be allowed to soak into the ground (ibid.). Sometimes, grains are mixed with the blood, and those that sprout in it are considered auspicious for the next planting (Whitehead 1921, pp. 64–65). It would appear, then, that the goddesses are identified with the earth, which, through drinking the blood, vitalizes the crops and feeds the herds. The importance of women (an agent of procreation) in the worship of the Seven Sisters/Virgins may also have a connection with fertility.

Second, in some ceremonies, the protection of children, cattle, etc. is explicitly regarded as the main aim, as we have seen above. That the protection of the village is also a main aim is indicated by the way boundary locations are involved in many ceremonies. Evil occurrences, such as an epidemic, are often regarded as indicative of demons' invasion of the village from outside (Kinsley 1986, p. 205).

Such evil occurrences, however, may also be considered a manifestation of the goddesses' anger aroused by the villagers' neglect of them (a good example is given in Fawcett 1890, p. 270). Then, the ceremony held is of purgative nature. the purgative nature is also indicated by the sacrifice (whether it be the killing of animals, hook-swinging, or fire-walking). As Eliade put it:

> The ritual sending away of an animal ... or of a man ... [is] regarded as the material vehicle through which the faults of the entire community are transported beyond the limits of the territory it inhabits (1954, p. 53).

## 3.4 MEANING OF MULTIPLICITY

The above-discussed ceremonies for the Seven Sisters/Virgins could, perhaps, be seen as a means of restoring the village from the state of disorder or chaos into the state of order or integrity. As Harper (1977, pp. 68–69) notes, many ceremonies held on a yearly basis take place at the time of harvest, when the soil is exhausted and in a state of disorder, and the annual ceremonies are believed to 'renew the fertility of the land' (ibid., p. 69). Ceremonies of the purgative type, on the other hand, seek to annul the sins of the villagers (whether the sin of having neglected the goddesses, or the general sins accumulated over the past year) and to restore the village into the state of order and harmony. Thus, it would appear that the festivals in honour of the Seven Sisters/Virgins seek to renew the order and integrity of the village. Since, in chapter 2, we suggested that the number seven was associated with the power of cyclic renewal, it seems reasonable to ask: Could it be that this same number in aboriginal/Dravidian culture, too, is connected with cyclic renewal?

There are indications, provided by Harper (1977, pp. 47–54), that in this culture the number seven represents a type of completion or a transition into a higher order. Her material includes the following rituals involving the number seven. Certain ceremonial practices concerned with the first menses of a girl are performed in a manner indicative of her transition from childhood to womanhood and of her symbolic death and rebirth. Certain rites connected with the seventh month of pregnancy may indicate a death-to-life transition, for a fetus born before the seventh month of pregnancy almost always dies. Marriage ceremonies involving the number seven point to a new life whose primary purpose is reproduction. The death of a member of a family brings a seven-day period of pollution, during which all the members symbolically participate in death until they are reborn after the seventh day. Thus, it does look as though the number seven is a vehicle through which the renewal of the people can take place in Dravidian culture.

If we look again at the ceremonies held in honour of the Seven Sisters, we notice that one of the oft-found practices is the use of an oil lamp, whether on the severed head of a buffalo or on the heads of human participants (e.g. women who participate in fire-walking). This may be linked with the fact that, throughout the world, rites of renewal involve the extinguishing and ritual rekindling of fire (Eliade 1954, pp. 67ff).

In chapter 2, we discussed the cosmic significance of the number seven in the Vedic culture based on the Pleiades, etc. But unfortunately, we have no information on aboriginal observation of astronomical phenomena, other than the fact that the Santals of Bengal know the Pleiades, called *Sar en* (Harper 1977, p. 74). Yet, in the light of the importance of the Pleiades acknowledged in many primitive cultures throughout the world as the instrument for calculating agricultural calendars, Harper (ibid.) says that 'to hypothesize that the Seven Sisters or Virgins of aboriginal India are in some way related to the Pleiades is basically sound'[4] since the purpose of many ceremonies for the groups is yearly and agricultural renewal. At any rate, even though we cannot confirm the relation of the Seven Sisters to any natural or astronomical phenomena, it seems safe to suppose that the number seven is related to the notion of cyclic renewal or of the transition into a higher order.

Before closing this section, we may note in passing that the worship of the Seven Sisters/Virgins also often involves the notion that there is unity in multiplicity. We have come across Śītalā representing all the seven sisters. There are many other instances of the recognition of such unity of the seven. For instance, the underlying unity of the Seven Virgins associated with the Gingee Fort is not only stressed by Hiltebeitel's informants but also ritually affirmed (1988, p. 62). From the Telugu country, Whitehead, too, reported that his informants often said that the seven are 'only different names for the same goddess' (1921, p. 31).

---

4 We discussed the group of seven/six figures found in Indus seals. It may be worth noting here that there are some indications that Dravidian culure may have been related to the Indus Valley Civilization (Parpola 1985).

# 4. THE SAPTAMĀTṚKĀS

## 4.1 GENERAL DESCRIPTION

Scholars are generally agreed that the chthonic characteristics of the Mātṛs of the epic-Purāṇic literature suggest their aboriginal origins. The Saptamātṛkās may be linked to the aboriginal tradition, furthermore, through another important factor. As we have seen, the aboriginal/Dravidian culture regards the number seven as possessing great value and power, and the worship of the Seven Sisters/Virgins is prominent on the level of this particular culture throughout much of India. The Saptamātṛkās, however, also seem to be connected with the Vedic tradition as well. For one thing, the great value and power of the number seven was recognized also by this tradition; we have noted many Vedic heptads indicating this recognition. Further, chapter 2 presented some other, more specific connections between the Saptamātṛkās and the Vedic female heptads (e.g. seven wives having an illicit relationship with Agni). We have, thus, seen that the Saptamātṛkās may have been connected not only with the aboriginal goddesses but also with the Vedic female heptads—despite the latter's relatively mild nature. Thus, it would seem wise to suppose, with Harper (1977, p. 84), that the rise of the Saptamātṛkās in the epic-Purāṇic literature can best be seen as the result of mutual acculturation between, at least, these two traditions: aboriginal and Vedic (we have also considered the possibility that the constellation Pleiades was known to Indus Valley Civilization). Further, though we have looked at only heptads in aboriginal culture, other village goddesses—great numbers of them exist—may have been involved in this acculturation.

That this process of acculturation in, especially, the epic period was not smooth is indicated by the confused way in which the various groups of mothers appear in the Skanda-myths of the Mbh. While these myths make it reasonably clear that Skanda's father is Agni (or Rudra-Śiva assuming the guise of Fire), the Mbh 'obviously has not sorted out who should be the right mother of this new God', as van Buitenen says (1975, p. 207). The Mbh contains several different stories of the birth of Skanda. The *Vana Parva* (3.213ff) says that Svāhā, overcome with desire for Angi, assumed the shapes of the wives of the seven sages (for Agni was in love with these wives) and had intercourse with Agni. Svāhā was unable to assume the shape of Arundhatī because of her faithfulness to her husband and the power of her austerities. Svāhā, after each time she made love to Agni, put his seed in a golden basin in Mount Śvetā, all covered with reed stalks. The spilled seed eventually became Skanda. Agni is identified with Rudra, and Skanda is called Rudra's son at 3.218. 25ff. The *Śalya Parva* (ch. 44ff), on the other hand, explains that it was Śiva's seed that fell into a blazing fire, but that the energy was too great for Agni to bear. Agni threw it into the River Gaṅgā, who also was not able to bear the heat and threw the seed onto Mount Himavat. The six Kṛttikās found the child and nursed him. In the *Anuśāsana Parva* (ch. 85), Agni, identified as Rudra, makes love to Gaṅgā. She, however, cast off the burning seed in great distress. It then fell into a forest of reeds, in which it grew. The child was nursed by the presiding goddess of the Kṛttikās. The *Anuśāsana Parva* (ch. 86) also explains that Agni's seed, rejected by Gaṅgā, was divided into six portions, which then entered the Kṛttikās' wombs. This passage identifies Kārttikeya's father as Rudra.

Of these four stories, the *Vana Parva* account is the most complicated as far as groups of mothers are concerned. It is possible to discern at least three groups of mothers in this Parva. First, the gods, frightened by the great power of Skanda, sent 'all the Mothers of the world' to kill him (Mbh 3.215.10ff). Upon seeing Skanda, however, these Mothers both realized his invincible prowess and were taken over by their maternal nature. They said: 'You are our son. We hold the world. Welcome us all, we are yielding milk ...' (tr. van Buitenen 1975, p. 652). Only two of the Mothers are described in the text. One had been born from Fury. She guarded Skanda with a spike in her hand. The other, who was 'the cruel daughter of the blood sea [and] ... who feasts on blood' (tr. ibid.), embraced Skanda and guarded him like her son. A second group of mothers, referred to as 'maidens', are, along with lesser Kumāras, described as being born of Skanda when he was struck by Indra's thunderbolt (Mbh 3.217.1ff). It is, presumably, these maidens that are portrayed as the seven mothers in this same passage. These mothers ask Skanda to make them 'the ultimate Mothers of all the world' (tr. van Buitenen 1975, p. 653). These seven mothers are named Kākī, Halimā, Rudrā, Bṛhalī, Āryā, Palālā, and Mitrā. Their chthonic nature is clear not only from their association with the lesser Kumāras, who rob babies, both newborn and still in the womb, but also from the portrayal of each of the Mothers as having (by Skanda's grace) a 'most terrifying, red-eyed, and frightening son' (tr. ibid.). This marks the first occurrence, in literature, of a definitely chthonic septpartite group of females (Harper 1977, p. 89). We notice, in a later passage (Mbh 3.219.10ff), that the first band of mothers we saw above are unhappy that their position as the 'Mothers of the world' has been usurped by the 'seven mothers' and, further, that their progeny has been taken away by them. Therefore, they request of Skanda to restore these to them. These original 'Mothers of the world' also express their desire to devour the offspring of those other mothers. Skanda proposes that, though the progeny already given away cannot be returned, they are to be responsible for, and afflict, other children under sixteen. These mothers appear to be identified with the dreadful mothers called Graspers (Harper 1977, p. 90), who are described at Mbh 3.219.25ff. For instance, one of them enters a pregnant woman and eats the foetus, another feasts on children's flesh, another snatches small children, another aborts the foetuses, and so on. A third group consists of the seven sages' six wives, who were divorced on account of their alleged unfaithfulness (Mbh 3.219.1ff). The six, having come to Skanda, ask him to save them from this disgrace and to accept them as his mothers. He grants their requests. The six wives are also given a place in heaven as the constellation Kṛttikās. It is this group alone that has no dangerous nature in this account of the birth of Skanda.

A huge band of mothers is described in chapter 46 of the *Śalya Parva*, which gives 192 names and says that there are many more besides these. By looking at the *Śalya Parva* text, we see that many of these mothers were aboriginal goddesses that have been accepted into the Brahmanic pantheon, for the text stresses that these mothers have different ornaments, complexions, and languages. The text portrays their personalities as chthonic. The text says that these mothers live in trees, cross-roads, caves, and funeral grounds; that they are menacing in battle; and that they can magically disappear and change forms at will. This text, however, does not describe them as vicious and seems to recognize 'both … the beautiful and terrible … as … opposites of the same form' (Harper 1977, p. 93). Another noteworthy fact concerning this text is that it portrays some of the goddesses as partaking of the nature of gods. This Brahmanic portrayal, we might say, is something between the Vedic notion of females and wives of gods/sages, on one hand, and the more developed notion of females as the *śaktis* of gods (as in the Saptamātṛkās), one the other.

It seems fairly clear that the Mbh accounts of the mothers represent a transitional stage in which materials from different sources are in the process of merging with one another but have not yet developed fully into the form of the Saptamātṛkās. The number of mothers, their essential nature as gods' *śaktis*, and so forth, have not been finalized. The same state of confusion is observed in the icons of mothers dating from the second to fourth centuries CE—that is, around the time of the compilation of the later parts of the Mbh—as documented in detail by Harper (1977, pp. 94–116). The mothers' organization and affiliations with their corresponding male gods or with the flanking male gods have not yet been precisely determined. Later, when this group is standardized, it consists of Brahmāṇī, Māheśvarī, Kaumārī, Vaiṣṇavī, Vārāhī, Indrāṇī, and Cāmuṇḍā, and the group is usually flanked by Śiva (often in the form of Vīrabhadra) and Gaṇeśa (Panikkar 1988, p. 291).

It is the beginning of the fifth century CE that witnessed the first appearance of iconic groups positively identifiable as the Saptamātṛkās both within and outside the boundaries of the Gupta empire (Harper 1977, p. 113). For instance, there are two separate panels from Udayagiri, near Videśa, Madhya Pradesh (ibid., pp. 116–18; cf. Panikkar 1988, p. 292). These are placed in conjunction with Śaivite caves. They both consist of images of Viṣṇu, Gaṇeśa, and a Saptamātṛkā panel. I give some more examples from around this period. Dating from the second quarter of the fifth century is a Saptamātṛkā panel accompanied by an *ūrdhvaliṅga* Śiva (Harper

1977, pp. 120–21, Plate 14). Apart from Cāmuṇḍā, who is easily recognizable from her emaciated body, the other *mātṛs* are without any identifying attributes. This representation might contain one of the *vāhanas* of the goddesses.

It is in a set of Mātṛkās from Baroli (Harper 1977, pp. 122–24) that the *mātṛs* and Śiva are shown for the first time with definite *vāhanas* and attributes. Harper in her dissertation (1977) presents a detailed description of the century-by-century development of the Saptamātṛkā icons. We have no space here to recapitulate her long discussion; for our purposes, suffice it to say that, though the evolution of the Mātṛs into a standardized group of Saptamātṛkās seems to have taken place by the mid-fifth century, Harper (ibid., pp. 125) shows that a precise iconographic formula concerning each mother's attribute and *vāhana* lagged behind somewhat, and that it is in the sixth century that the Mātṛkās appear, for the first time, with their respective emblems, *vāhanas, and* children (ibid., p. 139). She also demonstrates that by the sixth and seventh centuries, icons of the Saptamātṛkās were worshipped throughout the Indian subcontinent (ibid., p. 113). Noteworthy examples of developed Saptamātṛkā icons are described by (in addition to Harper) T. A. G. Rao (1914, pp. 379ff), Panikkar (1988), Bhattacharyya (1974, pp. 102ff, 65), etc.

Before proceeding to look at literary material on the developed Saptamātṛkās, we may briefly note one important inscription dating from the fifth century CE. This inscription, dated 423–25, is from the village of Gaṅgadhār in western Malwa and says:

> ... for the sake of religious merit, the counsellor of the king caused to be built this very terrible abode ... (and) filled full of female ghouls [*ḍākinīs*], of the divine mothers,

who utter loud and tremendous shouts in joy (and) who stir up the very oceans with mighty wind rising from the magic [tantric] rites of their religion (quoted in Harper 1977, p. 119).

Though neither the number nor names of the mothers are mentioned, their close association with *ḍākinīs* and the magic rites is noteworthy. The cult of the mothers may have had some Tantric elements.

Turning to literary sources regarding the developed from of the Saptamātṛkās, we find that the earliest text to suggest the standardized iconographic forms of the Mātṛs is the *Bṛhatsaṃhitā*, which says, 'Mātṛs are to be made with cognizances of the gods corresponding to their names' (quoted in Tiwari 1985, p. 103). This text, however, does not specify their names, number, or *śakti* aspect. The earliest extant text to specify the names of the mothers and explicitly define their *śakti* aspect is the DM (ca. between the 6th and 8th centuries). However, the DM's list differs somewhat from the standard iconographic portrayal. The DM describes the following seven *śaktis* of male gods: Brahmāṇī, Māheśvarī, Kaumārī, Vaiṣṇavī, Vārāhī, Nārasiṃhī, and Aindrī (8.14–20). These *śaktis* are called *mātṛ-gaṇa* or Mātṛs (5.38; cf 5.44, 49). In addition, this text has another *śakti*, put forth not from any male god but from the Devī (Caṇḍikā) herself (DM 8.21–22). Since she engaged Śiva as messenger to summon the Aṣuras to battle, this *śakti* is called Śivadūtī (8.27). She is to be distinguished from another who emanates from Caṇḍikā, viz. Kālī (Cāmuṇḍā) (7.4ff). These *śaktis* essentially assist the Devī in fighting the Asurs. As pointed out by Coburn (1984, p. 315), these nine Mātṛs are regarded as a group, for they are praised in consecutive ślokas at DM 11.12–20 in the same order as they are described at 8.14ff. In addition, though the demise of Raktabīja is primarily attributed to Kālī, the other Mātṛs evidently share in her essential character, for they are portrayed, upon his death, as dancing and being intoxicated with his blood (8.62).

In Purāṇic literature, there seems to be a more or less standard form of myth of Mātṛs: They are conceived of as personified energies of seven (or eight) Brahmanical gods and as appearing to aid Śiva or the Devī in destroying Asura(s) (Tiwari 1985, p. 108). They fight ferociously and often become drunk with blood. A few more examples may be given. An account similar to the DM version is given in the *Vāmana Purāṇa* (30). An interesting variation here is that though the Mātṛs are named after the male deities as usual, they issue from different parts of the Devī's body (30.3–9). The DM version is repeated with little variation also in the *Devī-bhāgavata Purāṇa* (5.28–29). *Varāha Purāṇa*, too, gives a similar description of the Mātṛs, though the demon that multiplies with his blood touching the earth is named Andhakāsura (summarized in T. A. G. Rao 1914, Vol. I, Part II, pp. 379ff). The *śaktis* mobilized to prevent his blood from falling to the ground are the usual seven (viz. Brahmāṇī, Māheśvarī, Kaumārī, Vaiṣṇavī, Vārāhī, Indrāṇī, and Cāmuṇḍā) plus Yogeśvarī (Śiva's *śakti*). The usual group of seven also appears to perform a similar task to defeat Andhakāsura in the *Matsya Purāṇa* (179.9–32), though their names are followed by a long list of goddesses (about 190 names are given, but the text adds that there are many more) (Kinsley 1986, p. 158).

I end this section by summarizing the personalities of the Mātṛs. First, the Mātṛs of the transitional, epic period seem to be generally inimical and dangerous, with the possible exception of the Kṛttikās (or the six wives of the seven sages). Those inimical mothers are particularly dangerous to children. Second, descriptions of the fully developed Saptamātṛkās portray them primarily as assistants of the Devī (or Śiva) in fighting the Asuras—thus, bringing out something good about their character. Nevertheless, their dangerous, inimical, bloodthirsty character and terrible appearance are hardly suppressed (Kinsley 1986, pp. 158–60). In the *Matsya Purāṇa* account, for example, the Mātṛs, after slaying the demons, even proceed to devour all the gods and people of the world and end up having to be stopped by another band of goddesses (179.8–90). The *Varāha Purāṇa* (17.33–37) associates the Mothers with vices or inauspicious emotions, saying, 'Yogeśvarī is the symbol of lust, Māheśvarī of anger, Vaiṣṇavī of greed, Kaumārī of attachment, Brahmāṇī of pride, Aindrī of jealously, Cāmuṇḍā of depravity and Vārāhī of envy' (quoted in Kinsley 1986, p. 159). One other thing we ought tc note here is that, while literature thus describes the Mātṛs as terrible, inimical, and dangerous, iconography depicts elegant, graceful mothers (with the exception of Cāmuṇḍā), sometimes even with children. Could it be that such iconographical representations were more influenced by the tradition of the Kṛttikās and other, earlier Vedic Seven Mothers than by the aboriginal Seven Sisters?

## 4.2 THE FEMALES' RELATIONSHIP WITH MALES

One of the main characterizations of the Saptamātṛkās is to say that they are the energies of the male deities. This, coupled with these goddesses' names, appearances, and origins, could give the impression that the Saptamātṛkās are the mere consorts, or appendices, of the gods. The real idea behind all this, however, seems to be that the gods are inseparably associated with their *śaktis*, without whom they are actually powerless (Tiwari 1985, pp. 129–30). In fact, though the males need the females, the females do not seem to need the males. The DM account of the birth of Śivadūtī (8.22) shows that the Devī can produce a *śakti* without any male deity's help. In fact, there are indications that the *śaktis* can better be seen as extensions of the Devī, not of male deities. In the *Vāmana Purāṇa* account of the Mātṛ episode, for instance, the Mātṛs (though they are named and portrayed after the male deities) issue forth from different parts of the Devī's own body (30.3–90). Further, in the DM, when challenged by Śumbha to single combat, the Devī absorbs all the Mātṛs into herself, referring to them as her own different powers or forms (10.2–5). We may also note that we do not have significant information on the Mātṛs as spouses of their male counterparts.

## 4.3 MODE AND AIM OF WORSHIP/OTHER PRACTICE

Available material on this topic indicates that the worship of the Saptamātṛkās reflected their dangerous characters, which we have noted above. Thus, in the *Viṣṇudharmottara Purāṇa*, after Śiva defeats the demon Andhaka with the aid of the Mothers, there is a short chapter wholly devoted to certain rites by which the evil influences of the Mothers can be avoided (1.227). In the rite of the *Vṛddhi Śrāddha* described in the Purāṇas, etc., the Mātṛs are to be worshipped before the Pitṛs or other deities are worshipped because the Mātṛs would, otherwise, perpetrate violence (Tiwari 1985, p. 126). In protective rites for Kṛṣṇa described in the *Bhāgavata Purāṇa*, too, the cowherd women pray: 'May the Ḍākinīs, the Jatādhārīs, … the goblins, the Mātṛs … etc. [and] other evil omens and calamities … and other evil spirits be destroyed … ' (10.6.27–

29; quoted in Kinsley 1986, p. 159). One of the aims of the worship of the Saptamātṛkās, then, may have been to ward off their evil influences either through propitiation or exorcism.

There may have been another aspect to their worship, however. If the Mothers are symbols of bad mental qualities, as stated in the *Varāha Purāṇa* (17.33–37), then performing rites designed to propitiate the Mothers or to avoid their evil influences can mean keeping oneself from falling into evil states of the mind. Such rites, properly performed, will lead to a more enlightened way of life. This, then, may have been another of the aims of the worship of the Saptamātṛkās.

Another aim of worship may be noted: that is, to be blessed with progeny and to maintain the good health of offspring. This is suggested most clearly by the icons found at Mathura depicting mothers embracing children (Harper 1977, pp. 102–03, 184) but also by many other icons of graceful mothers with children. Further, the obtaining of offspring as the aim of worship of Mātṛs is recorded in secular literature such as Bāṇa's *Kādambarī* (ca. 600–650 CE), in which the Queen Vilāsvatī of Ujjayinī, who desired children, 'frequented the shrines of the Holy Mothers in the neighbourhood, which had given proof (by fulfilling the desires of the worshippers)' (quoted in Harper 1977, p. 185).

There are also indications that Tantric rituals may, at times, have been involved in their worship. We have already noted the Gaṅgadhār inscription referring to Tantric rites associated with the Mothers. In the *Bṛhatsaṃhitā* (first half of the sixth century), moreover, the Maga-Brahmana astronomer Varahamihira specifies that the Mothers are to be worshipped by the *mātṛ-maṇḍala-vidaḥ* or *maṇḍala-krama-vidaḥ* (Harper 1977, pp. 152–53). That the Mātṛ worship involved the use of the *maṇḍala* is also indicated by the *Devī Purāṇa* (ca. 550–650 CE) (ibid.).

## 4.4 MEANING OF MULTIPLICITY

In chapters 1 to 3, which dealt with elements that may have contributed to the formation of the Saptamātṛkās, we considered possible meanings of the number seven involved in groups of seven female deities. It has been seen that seven female deities may have represented the patterns of a cosmic totality, the cyclic renewal, the cyclic return to the original source of all, which is a new beginning of a higher order. In Vedic literature, this cyclic return to the original source seems to be indicated on various levels—such as that of music, visible colours, yearly renewal symbolized by the Kṛttikās, etc.—and these different levels may have been connected with one another in some way or other. Harper (1977, p. 181, etc.) believes that the basis for those heptads was the Kṛttikās. It has been seen in chapter 3 that the aboriginal groups of seven females may also represent similar rhythms of a totality or wholeness and cyclic renewal. Considering the agricultural significance of the *grāma devatās* and their rituals, one important form of the cyclic renewal, for the villagers, is the yearly re-creation of their agricultural land, which could have meant the whole universe to them.

There are no intrinsic reasons to suppose that these notions of cyclic renewal, or cyclic return to the original source (a new beginning), were not connoted also by the Saptamātṛkās (despite the fact that the conjunction of the Kṛttikās and the vernal equinox had long been gone by this time). However, the multiplicity of this fully developed form of the Saptamātṛkās may have had other meanings, as well. By far the most interesting suggestion in this respect has been made by Harper (1977, pp. 188ff), who says that the Saptamātṛkās represented a more *personal and spiritual* renewal—or a spiritual rebirth. The standard iconographical depiction of the Saptamātṛkās begins with Brahmāṇī, places Vaiṣṇavī in the middle (fourth) position, and ends with Cāmuṇḍā. Brahmāṇī, of course, is the power (*śakti*) of creation, Vaiṣṇavī the power of preservation, and Cāmuṇḍā the power of destruction. Thus, though the other four goddesses' meanings may be unclear, this group of seven seems to represent the three phases of being: birth, preservation, and death. Hence, to worship the Saptamātṛkās is to experience a symbolic, whole lifetime—that is, to die to one's old self and to start anew.

This interpretation of the meaning of the Saptamātṛkās as the spiritual or personal renewal accords with the fact that the various female heptads that we have looked at seem to symbolize a septpartite rhythm of the cosmic structure involving cyclic renewal and existing on various levels. It may be objected that the gap between the *cosmic* and *personal* structures would not allow the notion of cyclic renewal and septpartite nature (which we have seen as being part of the cosmic rhythm) to be applied to the personal structure. There is, however, something that connects the personal and cosmic septpartite structures. This connection is provided by the idea of the cosmicization of the body, through which the worshipper's body becomes the universe so that this microcosm can symbolically undergo the cosmic, cyclic renewal on a personal level, his body's septpartite structure now being indicated by such expressions as the seven *cakras* (ibid.). It might be objected, again, that the ideas of cosmicization and *cakras* are not part of the Mātṛ tradition. Yet, it would seem possible to connect these ideas with the

Mātṛs through the afore-mentioned association of the mothers with Tantric ritual. We remember that Varahamihira's instruction in his *Bṛhatsaṃhitā* recommends the *mātṛ-maṇḍala-vidaḥ* or *maṇḍala-krama-vidaḥ* as the mode of worship for the Saptamātṛkās. These terms may refer to the actual drawing of the mandala at a chosen place, but they could also indicate the internalization of the *maṇḍala*—a symbol of the cosmic cycle—within the body (Harper 1977, pp. 193–94). Further, this cosmicization process by means of the *maṇḍala* has a particular bearing on the *cakras*, for it is said: 'Viewed in projection the *cakras* constitute a *maṇḍala* whose center is marked by the *brāhmarandhra* [thousand petaled lotus, the final *cakra* to be realized]. It is in this "center" ... that passing beyond saṃsāra, "emerging from time" ... is accomplished' (Eliade 1958, p. 244). In addition, the *Śrī Kāmākhya Guhya Siddhi* places the following seven mothers in the *cakras*: from the top *cakra* downwards, Brāhmī, Māheśvarī, Vaiṣṇavī, Vārāhī, Aindrī, Cāmuṇḍā, and Mahālakṣmī (Dehejia 1986, p. 48). Though two of the mothers are different from the standard Saptamātṛkās, this text indicates that there was a tradition that located a variant of the Saptamātṛkās in the internal *cakras*.

Thus, it is not inconceivable that the Saptamātṛkās represented a personal, spiritual return to the original source (of all), a new beginning. This particular symbolical meaning of the Saptamātṛkās, incidentally, has some bearing on one of the aims of worship of this group of seven females that we noted above, viz. to progress towards a more enlightened way of living through dissociation from undesirable mental qualities that are represented by the seven Mothers.

Apart from this interpretation pointing to the notion of a

personal, spiritual renewal, however, the meaning of multiplicity of the Saptamātṛkās does not seem to permit of any other decisive interpretation.

# 5. THE LETTERS ( MĀTṚKĀS)

## 5.1 GENERAL DESCRIPTION

The term *mātṛkā* means both 'mother' and 'letters of the Sanskrit alphabet'. Thus, the *Vāmakeśvara Tantra* begins with the verse: 'I bow to the goddess who consists of mantra, who is the letters of the alphabet ...' (1.1; tr. Finn 1986, p. 155). In certain Tantras, such as the *Sānadātilaka* and the *Kāmadhenu Tantra*, the fifty letters of the alphabet are described as divine beings permeating the entire universe (Aryan 1980, p. 29). The *Kāmadhenu Tantra*, further, portrays the letters as having different colours and presents a 'detailed description of their diagrammatic forms, their Guṇas and powers' (ibid.).

To appreciate the full implications of the letters, however, one must understand them in their linguistic-cosmological-ontological sense, for one key idea in Tantrism is that speech, of which the letters are the smallest phonemic units, gives birth to the phenomenal world. Dyczkowski explains:

> The objective world of perceptions is ... essentially a chain of thought-constructs (*prapañca*) ... woven into the fabric of diversity.... This thought (*vikalpa*) is a form of speech (*vāc*) uttered internally by the mind (*citta*), which is itself an outpouring of consciousness. Consciousness also, in its turn, resounds with the silent, supreme form of speech (*parā vāc*) which is the reflective awareness through which it expresses itself to itself. Consequently, the fifty letters of the Sanskrit alphabet, which are the smallest phonemic units into which speech can be analysed, are symbolic of

> the principal elements of the activity of consciousness (1987, p. 185).

In other words, the fifty letters, from A to HA, can represent every phase of consciousness, which is the primary source of everything. So it can be said that the phenomenal world is constructed on letters. Thus, the *Vāmakeśvara Tantra* says, 'I give homage to her who is the sacred alphabet and whose letters the three worlds, from Brahmā to the lowest infernal region are threaded as on a great string' (1.5; tr. Finn 1986, p. 177). Kṣemarāja, too, says, 'The uncognized mother (*ajñātā mātā*), of this [threefold blemish] is Mātṛkā, [the "matrix"] who begets the world (*viśvajananī*) and whose form [is the verbal] cosmos extending] from "a" to "kṣa" ...' (quoted in Alper 1989, p. 273). Each of the letters has its own significance in this linguistic cosmogony, as explained by Hoens (1979, pp. 98ff). But we cannot go into such detail here.

Another way to look at the letters is suggested in the Tantras: that is, the letters are often classified into eight groups, each having its presiding mother. We read in the *Vāmakeśvara Tantra*: 'I worship Her in whom there is the presence of the Eight Mothers due to the arrangement of letters into classes, and who is the queen of the eight great *siddhis* which arise from (those) eight classes' (1.11; tr. Finn 1986, p. 187). In terms of the linguistic cosmology that we have noted, it is said that the rays of the phonemic energies, symbolized by the letters, emanate from Consciousness, the light of Śiva, in eight groups (Dyczkowski 1987, pp. 198–99). According to the *Svacchandabhairava Tantra*, the eight classes, their presiding deities, and the powers of the mental organ and the five senses that they represent are as follows:

*The Letters (Mātṛkās)*

| | | |
|---|---|---|
| Gutturals | Brāhmaṇī | Intellect (*buddhi*) |
| Palatals | Māheśvarī | Ego (*ahaṃkāra*) |
| Cerebrals | Khaumārī | Mind (*manas*) |
| Dentals | Ṇārāyaṇī | Hearing |
| Labials | Vārāhī | Touch |
| Semivowels | Āindrī | Sight |
| Sibilants | Cāmuṇḍā | Taste |
| Vowels | Mahālakṣmī | Smell |

(quoted in Dyczkowski 1987, p. 199)

The letters being regarded as symbolic of the activities of the universal Consciousness (as we have already noted), this group of eight mothers teaches the Tantric practitioner that the discursive workings of the mind and the five senses, which enable him to perceive the world, are in fact none other than emanations of Consciousness itself. However, ignorance of the true nature of the *mātṛkās* allows him to be bound by their negative powers, which brings him the sense of diversity (ibid.).

The philosophy involved in the tradition of the letters is extremely complex and worthy of deep investigation but, unfortunately, the limited space does not permit us to go into any more detail than we already have in the foregoing. We must remember that our primary purpose in this study is to understand the meaning of feminine multiplicity, the letters being one of the representative groups of multiple females.

## 5.2 THE FEMALES' RELATIONSHIP WITH MALES

Though there is a tradition that combines eight Bhairavas with the afore-mentioned eight mothers as *pīṭha* deities of Tripura

(Goudriaan 1979, p. 65), it is more often Śiva himself that is associated with the *mātṛkās*. While Śiva is universal Consciousness, the letters are emanations of the power (Hoens 1979, p. 97) without which the universe would not come forth into being (Singh 1977, p. 47). This power (Citi-Śakti), as the mother of the universe, contains within itself everything that is to come into existence just as a pregnant woman contains her child (Dyczkowski 1987, p. 198). Here we have two kinds of contrast. One is between the great multiplicity of females—fifty letters or eight classes—and the oneness of the male, Śiva. The other is between power and consciousness. Perhaps, we might say that it is this feminine power that can bring about this multiplicity of the feminine. The second kind of contrast, however, needs to be qualified somewhat, for, as Kṣemarāja says, the power is non-distinct from Śiva (Singh 1977, p. 47).

## 5.3 MODE AND AIM OF WORSHIP/OTHER PRACTICE

One of the primary aims, if not *the* primary aim, of the Tantric practice involving the *mātṛkās* seems to be to affirm the truth of the worshipper's identity with the deity (Wheelock 1989, p. 117). A clear indication of this point is the great mantra AHAṂ ('I'), for *a* is symbolically identified with Śiva and *h* with Śakti. Moreover, the affirmation, by this mantra, of the worshipper's identity with the deity is reinforced by the fact that the AHAṂ encapsulates the entire cosmos and leaves nothing out. *A*, the first letter of the Sanskrit alphabet, is the initial emergence of all the other letters and, thus, represents the Supreme, or the Absolute (*anuttara*). *Ha*, the final letter, denotes the state of completion in which all elements of experience are fully displayed. *Ha* 'is also the generative, emission (*visarga*) which, like the breath, casts the inner into the outer, and draws what is outside inward' (Dyczkowski 1987, p. 186). The combined A-Ha contains in it all the letters—which means, in the linguistic cosmogony we have discussed, that the A-Ha encapsulates every phase of universal Consciousness, or in other words, the cosmic outpouring (Śakti) which, again, flows back into the original source (Śiva). As Kṣemarāja says,

> Therefore the reality (*tattvam*) of the judgment 'I' (*ahaṃvimarśa*), which accounts for the efficacy of the great mantra (*mahāmantra-vīryātmano*), is this: The cosmos (*viśvam*) is simply that which is cocooned (*garbhikṛtam etad ātmakam eva*) by means of *pratyāhara*, between Śiva and Śakti, that is to say, between 'that beyond which there is nothing higher' (*anuttara*) and 'the unstruck sound,' [i.e., between a (*akāra*), the first letter of the Sanskrit alphabet, and *ha* (*hakāra*), the last, respectively] (quoted in Alper 1989, p. 279).

Another good indication that Tantric practice is designed to affirm the practitioner's identity with the deity is the Tantric *japa*. When the practitioner performs it, he internalizes the deity by envisaging her as identified with the complete set of Sanskrit letters and with his own self (Gupta 1979, p. 127). In addition, in the *nyāsa* stage of the rite of *ātmaśuddhi*, the practitioner accommodates the *mātṛkā* mantras, their seers, and ritual application within his body (ibid., p. 136).

Further, as we have noted above, the eight classes of the letters are said to represent the powers of the body's various means of perception, such as intellect, ego, mind, hearing, touch, etc. This means that the discursive workings of the human mind and the activities of the body's senses are really emanations of universal Consciousness. This symbolical meaning thus serves to affirm the practitioner's identity with Consciousness.

Another aim of the worship of the *mātṛkās* has been hinted at above: viz. the acquiring of *siddhis*, supernatural abilities. In fact, many written Tantric sources describe *siddhis* (Goudriaan 1979, p. 7). It must be noted that in Tantrism there is always a connection between the magical and the spiritual (ibid.). Tantrism seems essentially to be designed to weaken restrictive forces which prevent freedom—such as habitual reactive patterns rooted in identification with the limited. Benefits gained in Tantrism need not be restricted to the realm of the spiritual.

## 5.4 MEANING OF MULTIPLICITY

From the above discussion, it may be said, first, that the multiplicity of the letters is indicative of the power to bring about the great diversity that is all-encompassing and that constitutes the entire cosmos. Second, this multiplicity, at the same time, expresses the power to dissolve distinctions in time and space and to affirm this diversity's essential identity with the one, universal Consciousness. Thus, the *Vāmakeśvara Tantra* says:

> I bow to the great Goddess who as the alphabet is the Mother (and) supreme lady who stills the phenomenal distinctions arising in the vast wave of time progression (1.2; tr. Finn 1986, p. 168).

From the soteriological point of view, the multiplicity of the letters can be seen as at once binding and liberating. When the letters are split up and dispersed, they can give rise to obscuring forces that make one blind to one's essential identity with Consciousness. For instance, if the combination of letters '*ahaṃ*' is understood in that manner, it becomes the limited subjectivity 'I', i.e. the differentiated and separated consciousness, which can suffer the consequences of imagined separation from Consciousness—human imperfection. Thus, Kṣemarāja says:

> [She is the matrix] who imparts ... forms such as sorrow, astonishment, joy, and passion to cognitions that involve the appearance of various limited (*saṃkucita*) objects of cognition. [These cognitions] amount to the judgment (*parāmarśa*) that there has been an appearance, [i.e., that something is the case], irrespective of whether [that appearance] is 'predicative' or not (*avikalpakasa-vikalpaka*). [Examples of such judgments are] 'I am a performer of the *agniṣṭoma* sacrifice,' 'I am skinny' or 'I am fat,' [and] 'I am finite' (quoted in Alper 1989, p. 273).

However, the liberating power of the letters *is* there. When they are understood in their entirety—as phonemic energies symbolic of various phases of Consciousness—then their phonemic energies can return the differentiated consciousnesses to their one, original source. The AHAṂ, for instance, is then no longer a limited subjectivity but is none other than all that there ever is, in other words, universal Consciousness. Abhinavagupta, too, explains:

> When the [phonemic energies] are not known to be [em-

> anations of the Lord] they conceal the wonder … of consciousness which is the one essential non-discursive awareness [present throughout perception] and even in discursive thought. They obscure it with thought-constructs constituted by the diverse configurations of phonemes and syllables.… But once their true nature is understood correctly in this way, they bestow freedom in this very life.… This knowledge of their intimate being [at one with the absolute] consists of this, namely, that even in the midst of all these fluctuations, free at their inception of discursive representations, thought-constructs do not conjoin [individualized consciousness] with the wheel of energies consisting of the totality of phonemes … (quoted in Dyczkowski 1987, p. 199).

Thus, one important meaning of the multiplicity of the *mātṛkās* seems to be that this multiplicity represents the power to enable the practitioner, both, to experience diversity and to return to the *one*, essential, and all-embracing awareness, which is the source of everything. This multiplicity makes possible a return to the original unity, which is again a new beginning of diversity; but if the return has been truly realized, the diversity will no longer be a burden.

# 6. THE YOGINĪS

## 6.1 GENERAL DESCRIPTION

The Yoginīs, who usually come in groups of sixty-four or eighty-one, have been studied in great detail by Dehejia (1986). Mainly drawing on his material, we shall briefly look at some of their essential features, especially those that are relevant to our purpose of understanding feminine multiplicity.

I begin with a few remarks on the Yoginīs' origins. First, as shown by Dehejia (1986, pp. 67–77), iconographical and textual evidence indicates that what can positively be recognized as the Yoginī cult emerged around the ninth century CE though it would be wrong to suppose that it was totally unknown before that date. Second, the Yoginīs have their roots outside of the orthodox Brahmanical tradition (Dehejia 1986, p. 1). The Yoginī cult, involving Tantric ritual, magical spells, etc., may have developed from tribal and village cults (ibid.). Third, it is also worth noting that the cult of Yoginīs had connections with the cult of the Mātṛkās. The clearest indication pointing to such a connection is those lists of sixty-four Yoginīs that include the names of the Mātṛkās, such as found in the *Kālikā Purāṇa* (ch. 63), *Durgā Pūjā* DH/345, the *Mahākāla Saṃhitā*, the *Skanda Purāṇa*, etc. (ibid., pp. 194ff). A few other indications may be mentioned. The first verse of the *Vāmakeśvara Tantra* (ca. 11th century, Finn 1986, p. 45) says, 'I bow to the Goddess who consists of mantra; who is the letters of the alphabet; who takes the form of the lords of the *gaṇas*, the planets, the lunar mansions, the Yoginīs and the constellations, (and) who is the embodiment of the *pīṭhas*' (1.1; tr. ibid., p. 155). Commenting on this verse, Śrīmad Rājānaka Jayaratha quotes the following words of Naravāhanadatta:

'She is the origin of entities such as the yoginīs who are the mistresses of the signs of the zodiac and the lunar mansions, (and of) the lords of the planets who are the lords of the *gaṇas* a, ka, ca, ṭa, ta, pa, ya and sa' (ibid., p. 158).

In Purāṇic myths, moreover, the Yoginīs are sometimes placed side by side with the Mātṛkās. For instance, the *Skanda Purāṇa* (1.3.2.18–21) describes Pārvatī as having Durgā 'emit armies of Yoginīs and Mothers from her body' to kill Mahiṣa (O'Flaherty 1980, p. 314). Also interesting is the *Matsya Purāṇa* account of the terrible Mātṛkās, who, after defeating Andhaka for Śiva, had to be stopped from devouring the gods and people by another host of goddesses. The text says at the end of the episode that Śiva's terrible form as Bhairava was enshrined along with the icons of the Mātṛkās at the site of the battle (179.8–90; cited in Kinsley 1986, pp. 158–59). In iconography, it is usually Vīrabhadra, not Bhairava, that flanks (together with Gaṇeśa) the Saptamātṛkās, whereas at the centre of a Yoginī temple, there is normally a shrine for Bhairava (Dehejia 1986, p. 40). Thus, the enshrinement of Bhairava mentioned in this purāṇa may indicate that these terrible Mātṛkās might be understood as Yoginīs. We may note just one more indication of Yoginī–Mātṛkā connection. In the fifth-century (CE) site of Yoginī worship located at Samalaji in Gujarat, at least seventeen images of mother goddesses have been discovered, including the Saptamātṛkās, who are identifiable from their mounts, etc. (Dehejia 1986, p. 70). Some of the remaining figures hold a child, and one is a tribal goddess with a snake and a bear-skin garment. Such a grouping of Mātṛkās, which exceeds the standard number of mother goddesses in a single group, may suggest that the larger grouping of sixty-four Yoginīs may have developed from such early groups of multiple Mātṛkās.

In our discussion of the Mātṛkās, we noted some connections with Tantric ritual. The Yoginīs represented in Yoginī temples appear to have been patron deities of those who followed a Tantric path called Kaula (ibid., p. 31). Such Kaula texts as the *Kulārṇava*, the *Matottara Tantra*, and the *Kaulajñānanirṇaya* indicate that those who follow the Kaula path are the favourites of the Yoginīs, who bestow curses on those who oppose this path (ibid., p. 32). The Yoginī cult seems to have emerged as a branch of this Kaula school, known as Yoginī Kaula, which is described in the *Kaulajñānanirṇaya* as having been founded by Matsyendranātha (ibid.).

The Kaula ritual is said to involve the five *makāras*, which are offerings of fish, meat, grain, wine and ritual sexual union (Goudriaan 1979, p. 45). The ten early teachers of the Kaula school mentioned by Abhinavagupta are all said to have utilized wine, meat, and woman (Pandey 1963, p. 547). Through such *bhoga* (enjoyment), the practitioner of the Kaula school was to attain a state of bliss referred to as 'Kula' (ibid., p. 597). 'Kula is defined', says Dehejia, 'as a state in which the mind and sight are united, the sense organs lose their individuality and sight merges into the object to be visualized' (1986, p. 32). The term 'Kula' is also used to refer to Śakti as well as the Ultimate Reality itself; Śiva, in contrast to this Kula, is often called 'Akula' (Pandey 1963, p. 595). However, 'Akula' is also sometimes used for the Absolute (ibid.). The union of the two is said to give rise to the ultimate bliss (Dehejia 1986, p. 32).

The Yoginīs seem to have been visualized generally as a group of sixty-four, or sometimes eighty-one, forming a circle with Śiva (Bhairava) as the centre. They were envisaged as belonging to eight *kulas* (families) and were worshipped for protection and magical abilities by Kaula practitioners (ibid., pp. 33–35). The Yoginīs were believed to possess women, who then belonged to the *kula* of a higher maternal power (Sanderson 1988, p. 671). The eight major *kulas* are those of Brāhmī, Māheśvarī, Kaumārī, Vaiṣṇavī, Indrāṇī, Vārāhī, Cāmuṇḍā, and Mahālakṣmī (ibid., p. 671). These women possessed by the Yoginīs come into most intimate contact with the Kaula practitioners in rituals such as a Kaula Cakra (Dehejia 1986, p. 13).

The personality of the Yoginīs as a whole may seem ambivalent. A passage from the *Kulārṇava* says:

> Whether fierce or gentle, terrible to behold, all-powerful,
> Residing in the sky, on earth or in the vastness of space,
> May those Yoginīs always be well-disposed towards me
> (Quoted in ibid., p. 34).

But in regard to certain things, the Yoginīs can be quite hot-tempered. For instance, the above text states that those who have the capacity to perform a Kaula Cakra but do not perform it will be destroyed by the Yoginīs, and that those who make caste distinctions in this ritual will be eaten by the goddesses (ibid.). The same text and the *Kaulajñānanirṇaya* contain warnings against insulting women and becoming angry with women even if they have a fault (ibid.). Many Yoginīs have a decidedly chthonic nature. Some texts describe the Yoginīs as fond of drinking blood and wine while eating the flesh of animals, and such a personality is evident from names of some of these Yoginīs. Another thing we may note about the character of the Yoginīs is that they are believed to assume the forms of various animals, birds, and humans (ibid.). Many icons of the

Yoginīs have the head of an animal, bird, or some creature or other. This aspect of the Yoginīs may be connected with the Mātṛs of the *Śalya Parva* (ch. 46), who are also said to assume any form at will.

The cult of the Yoginīs must have been fairly influential as indicated by the many Yoginī temples which still exist. Some of them are finely constructed and carved, and this suggests possible royal support for this cult. Temples of the Yoginīs are certainly amongst the most important features of this cult. The Yoginī temples are architecturally very different from other shrines in India. Though there are a few rectangular temples, the Yoginī temple is generally circular in shape with the sixty-four, or eighty-one, or occasionally forty-two, niches placed on the circumference, each containing an image of a Yoginī. All the temples are hypaethral, or open to the skies, have no tower, and are enclosed by stone walls which are usually plain on the exterior (Dehejia 1986, pp. 39–40). At the centre of the circle, there is, as we have noted, a shrine dedicated to Bhairava (ibid., pp. 35, 40).

## 6.2 THE FEMALES' RELATIONSHIP WITH MALES

In regard to the female–male relationship, it might seem significant that Bhairava's shrine takes the central location in a Yoginī temple. The Kaula texts suggest that Bhairava was visualized at the centre of the circle of Yoginīs (Dehejia 1986, p. 35). But there are other ways to associate the Yoginīs with Śiva. For instance, in one form of the Khecarī Cakra of sixty-four Yoginīs, it is Śiva and Śakti that are at the centre of the Cakra (envisaged in the form of a lotus flower) and are surrounded by successive layers of lotus petals (ibid. p. 44). The overlapping of the two triangles at the centre suggests a state of union of Śiva and Śakti. Another kind of Yoginīs' association with males is found in the Yoginī Cakra, whose sixty-four Yoginīs are totally different from those of the Khecarī Cakra (ibid., p. 45). These Yoginīs are derived in sets of eight from female deities, and each of the eight groups is associated with a Bhairava, who is portrayed as sporting with the Yoginīs. Some texts, moreover, even enumerate sixty-four Bhairavas in eight groups of eight each as consorts or guardians of the sixty-four Yoginīs (Banerjea 1956, p. 465). Earlier, we also noted that it is the union of Śiva and Śakti that is said to give rise to the ultimate bliss (Dehejia 1986, p. 32).

The importance of Śiva in the Yoginī cult is evidently acknowledged. It is, however, the male that is envisaged as *human* as opposed to the *divine feminine* since, as we shall see below, the practitioner identifies himself with Śiva in ritual enactment of this union.

## 6.3 MODE AND AIM OF WORSHIP/OTHER PRACTICE

We have already noted the five *makāras*, which culminate in sexual union in a Yoginī Cakra. In this formation, each initiate, regarded as Śiva, is accompanied by a female partner, a human representative of a Yoginī (Dehejia 1986, p. 13). Though the five *makāras* do not include blood, texts emphasize the importance of the offering of blood, as well as meat, in the worship of the Yoginīs.

We have also mentioned some diagrams used for worship. Such diagrams seem to have been an earlier tool of worship than temples (ibid., p. 43). In addition to those diagrams already mentioned, there are several other *cakras*, such as the Mūla Cakra of Eighty-One Yoginīs and the Bhūtalipi Cakra of Forty-Two Yoginīs.

The Yoginīs were also worshipped in rituals involving corpses as mentioned in several texts, notably, the *Matottara Tantra*, which presents details of such a ritual (ibid., pp. 58–61).

Not all Yoginī worship was external. As indicated by a later chapter of the *Matottara Tantra*, the Yoginīs could be located internally in such a way that each of the eight groups is given an internal place associated with one of the eight sacred towns, *kṣetra* (ibid., p. 48).

We said in chapter 5 that many Tantric texts are interested in describing magical powers to be obtained through practice. This seems particularly relevant to the Kaula texts, as shown by Dehejia (ibid., pp. 53–56), for they do seem to stress a variety of magical abilities to be acquired. Dehejia even says that salvation as such was not the aim of Yoginī worship (ibid., p. 53). As we noted earlier, however, Tantrism usually maintains some connecting thread between the spiritual and the magical, and this seems to apply to the Yoginī cult as well. As Sanderson (1988, pp. 679–80) says, the Yoginī Kula rituals seem, ultimately, to be designed to affirm the practitioner's inner, trans-individual identity as the blissful, enlightened Consciousness.

## 6.4 MEANING OF MULTIPLICITY

The majority of Yoginī temples contain sixty-four Yoginīs, and a few temples contain eighty-one Yoginīs. There are, however, also two known temples of forty-two images of Yoginīs (Dehejia 1986, pp. 141–44), and we have also mentioned the Bhūtalipi Cakra of Forty-two Yoginīs. The number forty-two can be regarded as an auspicious number because the number of the Tantras in certain schools is forty-two and the Śakti *pīṭhas* are sometimes considered to number forty-two (ibid., p. 51). Dehejia also suggests—based on the fact that the term 'Bhūtalipi' refers to a specialized arrangement of forty-two of the fifty Sanskrit letters—that this *cakra* and the forty-two-Yoginī temples were designed to accommodate these forty-two personified letters (ibid., pp. 51–52).

The principal number for the Yoginīs, however, is certainly sixty-four. One possible explanation of this number is to say that it is a multiple of the traditionally important number four—e.g. the Vedas speak of the four main directions (Dehejia 1986, p. 43). Though the number eight and its multiples are very important, the twelve petals of the Khecarī Cakra described in the *Matottara Tantra* cannot be accounted for by that number but is a multiple of four.

On the whole, however, the number eight seems to have been given much greater significance in the Yoginī cult than the number four since some texts explicitly describe the Yoginīs as 'eight times eight deities', 'eight Kulas and the sixty-four', 'eight groups of eight', etc. (ibid., p. 34). In addition, many *cakras* for the Yoginīs are graphic representations of the formation of the eight sets of eight goddesses (e.g. ibid., pp. 43, 46, 47, etc.). Eight was, in fact, another traditionally important number in India, and Dehejia cites various groups of eight (ibid., pp. 43–44). If eight was an auspicious number, its square can be even more powerful.

Moreover, as we have seen, eight is the number of the classes of the Sanskrit letters, each class having its presiding Mother. Not only do many lists of Yoginīs contain these Mothers (ibid., pp. 194ff), but the *Agni Purāṇa* explicitly derives the Yoginīs from this set of eight Mothers: Brahmāṇī, Māheśvarī, Kaumārī, Vaiṣṇavī, Vārāhī, Aindrī, Cāmuṇḍā, and Mahālakṣmī (ibid., pp. 34, 187) (though the list of the eight class deities of the Sanskrit letters that we noted earlier mentions Nārāyaṇī in place of Vaiṣṇavī). We have also seen some other indications of the connections between the Yoginīs and the Mothers earlier. It would seem safe, then, to suppose that there was a tradition that derived the Sixty-four Yoginīs from the eight presiding Mothers of the eight classes of the Sanskrit letters, though the eight divisions of the sixty-four Yoginīs are not always associated with the names of those particular eight Mothers (e.g. the Yoginī Cakra described in the *Matottara Tantra*—ibid., p. 47).

Next, inasmuch as the sixty-four Yoginīs are visualized or depicted, most of the time, in the form of a circle,[5] one should also consider Yoginīs' multiplicity in conjunction with the symbolical meaning of a circle. In India traditionally, the use of a circle (or *maṇḍala*) seems to point to spiritual, as well as magical, concerns. As we have said, though early texts concerned with the Yoginīs seem mainly preoccupied with description of the magical abilities, we need not suppose that the devotees of the Yoginīs had no interest in spiritual benefits at all. Such spiritual concerns on their part are indicated by the afore-mentioned connections with the eight mothers representing the eight classes of the letters, whose multiplicity is, as we have seen, symbolic of the emanation and withdrawal of the one original source of all from and back into itself. Regarding the *maṇḍala*, Beane, with Eliade, interprets the *maṇḍala* as having two functions. It is equivalent to an initiation ritual, and it protects the individual, enhances concentration, and helps him to find his own centre (1977, p. 207). Beane says, further, that the use of the *maṇḍala*—which is symbolic of the deity and of the cosmic manifestations pouring from and flowing back to the primordial unity—may be considered an attempt to affirm the individual's oneness with the universal Self and the deity (ibid., p. 208). The two forms of the Khecarī Cakra given in the *Matottara Tantra* and described

[5] Some texts even say that their worship without a *maṇḍala* is fruitless (Dehejia 1986, p.). Besides, most Yoginī temples are circular.

by Dehejia (1986, pp. 44, 45), for instance, graphically represent the unfolding, from the primordial unity-centre, of the sixty-four Yoginīs. At the same time, they can be viewed as symbolic of the reverse process back into the original source, with which the individual identifies himself in mystical experience (ibid., p. 43).

Lastly, a word has to be said about the eighty-one Yoginīs. Some textual material indicates that the number 'eighty-one' may be conceived of as the square of 'nine' (ibid., pp. 48–49), which again is an auspicious number, as we shall see in more detail in a later chapter on the Nine Durgās. However, it may also be possible to regard this Yoginī formation based on nine as a variation of the usual formation based on the number eight. The Mūla Cakra, as described in the *Matottara Tantra*, revolves around the concept of the nine Mātṛkās (here understood as Yoginīs) who are essentially the eight Mātṛkās (of the letters) plus Caṇḍikā (ibid., p. 48). Further, each of the nine Mātṛkās gathers around herself *eight* Yoginīs, who are graphically represented as the *eight* lotus petals surrounding each of the nine major Yoginīs. Thus, it may be that the group of eighty-one Yoginīs was a special variation of the sixty-four Yoginīs. In fact, this group seems to have been considered primarily suited for royal temple construction (ibid., pp. 49–51).

# 7. DEITIES OF THE ŚRĪ-CAKRA

## 7.1 GENERAL DESCRIPTION

Again, this is a complex topic, and I can only summarize certain essential characteristics of the Śrī-Cakra that are the most pertinent to us. The Śrī-Cakra is used for the worship of the Devī, variously referred to as Lalitā, Tripurā-Sundarī, Ṣoḍaśī, etc. (S. K. R. Rao 1989, p. 2). Its main components are (from the outer to the inner) a great square with four doors; six concentric circles within the square (the fifth and sixth being decorated with lotus petals and leaves); nine interpenetrating triangles, five with the top downwards and four with the top upwards; and a dot at the centre, called *bindu* (Hoens 1979, p. 114).

The central *bindu* represents the union of the ultimate male principle (Śiva, or consciousness) and the ultimate female principle (Śakti, or energy) (S. K. R. Rao 1989, p 14). The triangles symbolize the differentiated male and female principles, the ones with their apex upwards indicating the male and those with their apex downwards the female (ibid.). But the way in which the triangles interpenetrate indicates that the two principles cannot totally be separated. As Śivānanda points out, the real nature of the Śrī-Cakra is always the undivided essence of Śiva and Śakti who are the source (*bīja*) of subject/object distinctions (Brooks 1987, p. 281). The unified Brahman undergoes no change in order to assume the binary form of Śiva and Śakti, who are only distinguished as such on the level of the ordinary epistemological dualism (ibid.). It is only from the theological, cosmological, or ritualistic perspective that one speaks of the Śrī-Cakra as representing the creation coming forth from the *bindu* (focal point of non-dual consciousness). Then, the

Śrī-Cakra can be approached in two ways: purely cosmological and theoretical analysis sees creation as coming forth from the central *bindu* and evolving into greater and greater forms of diversity and discursive reality as one moves outwards. In contrast, the ritual practices lead the practitioner back to the original source of being by dissolving the limited, dualistic subjectivity into undifferentiated, non-dual consciousness (Brooks 1987, p. 280).

This latter approach dissolves the manifold back into the One. Here, the Śrī-Cakra can be envisaged, in mythological terms, as an elaborate mansion, in whose innermost apartment abides the Goddess. (Though the central *bindu* represents the union of the Śiva and Śakti, this theology describes the female as the predominant aspect—the male is merely a cot on which the Goddess rests (S. K. R. Rao 1989, p. 14)). This mansion contains a series of nine concentric enclosures (centring on the *bindu*), and it is only by passing through them that the practitioner can reach the sanctum. These enclosures both hide the divine presence and illumine the practitioner's path (ibid., p. 16). True, these enclosures cover the central deity by phenomenal and psychical projections. But they are also inseparably linked with the central *bindu* (as visually shown by the diagram) and, thus, they are instructive of the nature of the creation as cosmological emanations of the One. Further, the goddesses inhabiting the enclosures are considered representative of different aspects of the Devī of the *bindu*, as we shall see below.

For our purposes, one of the important features of the nine enclosures is that each has 'its presiding divinity (*chakra-nāyikā* or *chakreśvarī*) who is a variant form of the mother-goddess abiding in the central point, a class of specific aides in the spiritual progress of unification (*yoginīs*) representing different aspects of the mother-goddess, and a particular seal-divinity (*mudrā-devatā*) who welcomes, purifies and delights the devotee ...' (ibid., p. 26). Let us briefly look at some of the prominent deities of these enclosures as described in the Śrī-Vidyā tradition (based on Brooks 1987, pp. 285–322, unless otherwise indicated).

The first enclosure, the outermost gateways of the Śrī-Cakra, has twenty-eight *yoginīs* in three groups assigned to specific locations on each of its three lines. The first group of ten *yoginīs* embody the ten supernatural accomplishments (*siddhis*). The second group of *yoginīs* assigned on the second line, also called the *mātṛkās*, are the same as the eight Mothers presiding over the eight classes of the Sanskrit letters. The ten *yoginīs* of the innermost line are identified with the ten *mudrās*.

The second enclosure has sixteen *yoginīs* on its sixteen lotus petals, associated with sixteen vowels of the Sanskrit alphabet (S. K. R. Rao 1983, p. 86). These goddesses, whose names indicate powers of attraction, are primarily considered to represent worldly achievements and powers. The third enclosure includes eight lotus petals associated with eight groups of consonants and is inhabited by eight *yoginīs* connected with the 'principle of erotic urges independent of the physical body, and differentiated by the several functions of attraction' (ibid., pp. 89–90). The fourth enclosure consisting of fourteen triangles has fourteen *yoginīs*, who are specifically called *śaktis*, powers. These powers represent the central Devī's fourteen powers, which preside over the fourteen principal channels of the body (ibid., pp. 93–94). The fifth enclosure's ten triangles represent ten powers of the Devī which are called 'provider of all attainments' (ibid., p. 97). These powers are symbolized by ten *yoginīs*, whose names reflect mundane qualities. The sixth enclosure, too, has ten triangles representing ten powers of the Devī and inhabited by ten *yoginīs*. The seventh enclosure has eight *yoginīs* in its eight triangles, and the eighth enclosure is inhabited by three forms of the Devī: Kāmeśvarī, Vajreśvarī, and Bhagamālinī (ibid., p. 112).

In sum, what attracts our attention most strongly here is that these deities of the Śrī-Cakra—which, as we have noted, represent different aspects of the Devī—seem to be connected mostly with some kind of power or other of the Devī presiding over the whole Cakra.

## 7.2 THE FEMALES' RELATIONSHIP WITH MALES

Suffice it to say that, though the male and female principles are considered inseparable, the superior position is evidently given to the female. As Brooks says (1987, p. 283), Śakti plays her role 'as that aspect encompassing both material and causal powers and as the Self reflecting (*vimarśa*) the illuminative (*prakāśa*), immobile Brahman'. The male is regarded as entirely inert like a corpse without his śakti.

## 7.3 MODE AND AIM OF WORSHIP/OTHER PRACTICE

The complex ritual procedures involving the Śrī-Cakra have been documented by such scholars as Brooks (1987) and Gupta (1979). I shall simply note one aspect that concerns us directly. That is, (as we have seen above) the practitioner is ritually to pass through a series of enclosures and reach the innermost chamber of the deity presiding over the whole of the Śrī-Cakra. His aim is identification with this deity, who however is not different in substance from creation, which is the deity's own emanations.

## 7.4 MEANING OF MULTIPLICITY

From the above, it would appear that the meaning of multiplicity of the Śrī-Cakra can be seen as two-fold. First, as the above cosmological analysis and summary of goddesses of the series of enclosures indicate, the multiplicity of the Śrī-Cakra expresses a variety of different aspects, particularly various powers, of Śakti which, through reflecting the illuminative, immobile Śiva, enables the macrocosmic Consciousness to bring itself into manifold, particular forms. Second, this multiplicity, however, is also designed to return the manifold to the One, as in ritual practices.

# 8. THE TWELVE KĀLĪS

## 8.1 GENERAL DESCRIPTION

The Krama tradition absorbed in the Trika sets forth five systems of wheels (*cakra*) of power emanating from the essential cosmic Consciousness, each system being a description of the manifestation and return of Consciousness from and back into itself (Flood 1988, pp. 149–51). It is the last of these five systems that concerns us. This is the system of the five powers: emanation (*sṛṣṭi*), maintenance (*sthiti*), destruction (*saṃhāra*), the nameless (*anākhya*), and the brilliant (*bhāsa*)—each of these, again, having sub-systems. The system of the Twelve Kālīs is one of these sub-systems classified under the 'nameless' and is, itself, a complete account of the essential Consciousness emanating from and withdrawing back into itself (ibid., p. 152). The importance of the system of the Twelve Kālīs is indicated by the fact that all the other wheels of power emerge from it and also eventually are dissolved in it (Dyczkowski 1987, p. 124; Flood 1988, pp. 152ff).

The Twelve Kālīs, which radiate from the hub of the wheel, represent the manifest cosmos, while the hub is considered by Abhinavagupta and the Krama tradition to be Kālasaṃkārṣiṇī (destroyer or attractress of time) as the essential cosmic body. The *Jayadrathayāmala Tantra* also refers to the centre of the wheel as Mahākālī (Great Kālī). Details of the Twelve Kālīs are presented by Pandey (1963, pp. 513–21) and Flood (1988, pp. 156–57). The twelve are different from Mahākālī (or Kālasaṃkārṣiṇī) in their names but are envisaged as identical in appearance (Sanderson 1988, pp. 676–77) and iconographically depicted in that way (Flood 1988, p. 158). Essentially, what this system expresses, then, is the perfect identity in substance of the universal Consciousness and its manifestations. Kālasaṃkārṣiṇī projects herself as the Twelve Kālīs, who represent the manifest universe, and withdraws them back into herself, which is a state of non-duality and non-differentiation. Not only is this wheel a way of accounting for the emanation and withdrawal of Consciousness, but it is also 'a means of liberation in so far as they devour duality and the illusion of an individual consciousness distinct from Kālasaṃkārṣiṇī or the Nameless (*anākhya*)' (Flood 1988, p. 153).

The wheel of the Twelve Kālīs represents a number of specific things, such as the twelve senses (i.e. the intellect, the mind, the five organs of knowledge, and the five organs of action), the twelve vowels of the Sanskrit alphabet, and different phases in the cognitive cycle (Dyczkowski 1987, p. 124). In this last instance, the Twelve Kālīs are divided into three stages of emanation (or three groups of four Kālīs): the object, means, and subject of cognition (Flood 1988, p. 155). According to Abhinavagupta, the twelve Kālīs in fact represent the totality of manifestation and reabsorption and are present in all appearances (ibid., p. 156).

## 8.2 THE FEMALES' RELATIONSHIP WITH MALES

As the wheel of the Twelve Kālīs is generally understood, it is dominated, as we have seen above, by feminine power and does not seem to involve anything of the masculine. True, Kṣemarāja transposes Kālasaṃkārṣiṇi with Bhairava as the essential cosmic principle, saying that he (the hub of the wheel) causes exertion, appearance, tasting, and destruction through the cycle of the Twelve Kālīs (Flood 1988, pp. 152–53). But this way of looking at this group of Kālīs does not seem very common and might even be regarded as an exception. We may, however, note that in Kṣemarāja's interpretation, too, the *power* enabling the cosmic processes to proceed is attributed to the females.

## 8.3 MODE AND AIM OF WORSHIP/OTHER PRACTICE

The practice involving this group of Kālīs, as stated in the *Jayadrathayāmala Tantra*, may involve orgiastic rites, while 'the thirteen Kālīs (12+1) are to be realized internally in mystical self-experience, flashing forth as the ego-less ... void through the voids of the senses during sexual union with the *dūtī*' (Sanderson 1988, p. 677). Or the practice may be done purely internally through paying close attention to the pulsing of the wheel of the Twelve Kālīs during each act of cognition as Kālasaṃkārṣiṇī projects herself out as the Twelve Kālīs and withdraws them back into herself—or, in metaphysical terms, as universal Consciousness emanates itself from the centre of purity and non-duality towards the periphery, which constitutes the manifest and the manifold, and then returns itself to itself. The practitioner, then, comes to see that all is generated through, and contained within, the cycle of Consciousness. To put this another way, since the Twelve Kālīs are considered to represent different, successive phases of Consciousness's movement, beginning with projection of existence (first Kālī) and ending with the reabsorption of all (twelfth Kālī), so the manifestation of the Kālasaṃkārṣiṇī as twelve forms is, as Abhinavagupta says, envisaged in succession and the final liberation is attained when the last Kālī is realized (Pandey 1963, p. 513).

## 8.4 MEANING OF MULTIPLICITY

What is the meaning of the feminine multiplicity as found in this particular wheel of power (*śakticakra*), the wheel of the Twelve Kālīs? First, the number twelve itself does not seem to be given any intrinsic significance here. Though we have been looking at only the Twelve Kālīs, various numbers have traditionally been used in the grouping of the Kālīs for the wheel of power under the 'Nameless' (*anākhya*). Some texts within the Krama tradition, for instance, list thirteen Kālīs (e.g. the *Pañcaśatika*, the *Tantrarāja*, and the *Sārdhaśatika*—Pandey 1963, p. 521). One text (the Krama *Sadbhāva*) even includes seventeen goddesses (ibid.). Pandey, therefore, says that there was no fixity about the number of the Kālīs in this wheel of power (ibid., p. 522).

Second, if we cannot say anything about specific numbers used in the formation of this wheel, our brief description of the Twelve Kālīs above still yields some significance of the multiplicity of the Kālīs of our wheel. That is, this multiplicity instructs the practitioner in the fundamental, perfect identity of diversity and unity, or of manifestations and their source. As we have seen, the Twelve Kālīs symbolize the emanation and withdrawal of the essential cosmic Consciousness from and back into itself, the twelve being envisaged as identical in essence to the central deity. Put more mythologically, this wheel tells of Kālasaṃkārṣiṇī projecting herself as the Twelve Kālīs and reabsorbing them back into herself. Needless to say, this process is a pulsating movement in the context of the tradition we are concerned with, repeated over and over—which means that the reabsorption of manifestations into their source denotes a new beginning of another cycle.

## 9. THE NINE DURGĀS

### 9.1 GENERAL DESCRIPTION

There are various lists of Nine Durgās, including some noted by Banerjea (1956, pp. 490n1, 500) and another presented by Kumar (1974, p. 232). Two of these lists form part of the sixty-four Yoginīs contained in the *Kālikā Purāṇa*. Each name in another list contains the term *caṇḍa*, meaning 'fierce or wrathful' and indicating a fierce aspect of Durgā (Dehejia 1986, p. 188). Another list of Nine Durgās seems to sketch a series of major events in the life of Pārvatī—this list goes: Śailaputrī (daughter of the mountains), Brahmacāriṇī (unmarried one, referring to her performance of penance to obtain Śiva as husband), Caṇḍaghaṇṭā, Kusmāṇḍā, Skandamātā (mother of Skanda), Kātyāyanī (descriptive of the form in which she killed the buffalo-demon), Kālarātrī, Mahāgaurī, and Siddhidātrī (giver of perfection) (ibid.).

One of the most important sets of Nine Durgās is perhaps the one that is associated with the Navapattrikā (nine plants) ceremony of the autumnal Durgā worship in Bengal (Kane 1974, Vol. V, Part I, pp. 163–64; Kinsley 1986, pp. 111–12). The nine goddesses identified with the nine different plants are: Brahmāṇī, Kālikā, Durgā, Kārttikī, Śivā, Raktadantikā, Śokarahitā, Cāmuṇḍā, and Lakṣmī (Banerjea 1956, p. 490n1). Some of these nine plants are agricultural plants, such as plantain and paddy. Perhaps, this association of the Nine Durgās with these plants suggests Durgā's identification with 'power inherent in all vegetation' (Kinsley 1986, p. 111; also a similar suggestion given by Banerjea 1956, p. 490).

In iconography, according to the *Skandayāmala* (summarized by T. A. G. Rao 1914, pp. 356–57), one of the Nine Durgās is set up in the middle surrounded by the other eight. The central figure is eighteen-armed, is adorned with various ornaments, and has big breasts and thighs. She can grant all powers. She rides on a lion and holds the hair of the Asura emerging from the cut-end of the neck of Mahiṣāsura. The surrounding eight goddesses are sixteen-armed and seated on *rathas* shaped like lotuses. In colour, the central Durgā is like fire, while the others are yellow, red, black, blue, white, gray, turmeric-yellow, and pink. The names of these powerful Nine Durgās conform to the afore-mentioned list in which each of the nine names contains the term *caṇḍa* (fierce or wrathful). Banerjea (1956, p. 500) mentions icons that were recovered in a North Bengal village in the district of Diknajpu. These icons, too, accords, in the main, with this description.

## 9.2 THE FEMALES' RELATIONSHIP WITH MALES

From the above account, it may be said that the Nine Durgās are really *either* multiplied manifestations of Durgā as Mahiṣāsuramardinī (Slayer of Mahiṣāsura) *or* symbols of the power underlying all vegetation. But the latter group does not seem to be associated with any males. In the present section, therefore, I restrict myself to summarizing Mahiṣāsuramardinī's relationship with males. As described in the DM, Durgā emerges out of the male deities to defeat the Asuras because the males were unable to do so themselves. She obtains weapons, mounts, etc. from the male deities. This male–female power relationship points clearly to female dominance.

There are also indications, from village goddess worship, that Durgā's slaying of Mahiṣāsura may be attributable to male aggression and unjust mistreatment suffered by the female. But we cannot go into detail about it here. We shall have occasion to address this theme later.

## 9.3 MODE AND AIM OF WORSHIP/OTHER PRACTICE

As we have mentioned above, the Nine Durgās seem to have been worshipped sometimes through icons. There is, however, not much information on the aim of this form of worship, except that the central Durgā is described in the *Skandayāmala* as capable of granting all powers (noted above). Gaining powers, then, was probably one of the aims of the worship.

We know that the Nine Durgās are worshipped in another way. That is, they are identified with the nine different plants in the autumn Durgā Pūjā and, during their worship in this form, they are anointed with water from auspicious sources and with agricultural products besides receiving certain soils associated with fertility (Kinsley 1986, p. 111). The aim of this form of worship, then, seems to be the promotion of fertility of crops, for these Nine Durgās, as we have noted, clearly represent the power underlying all vegetation.

## 9.4 MEANING OF MULTIPLICITY

First, the number nine seems to be another auspicious number for ritual worship. There are, of course, the nine nights (*navarātrī*) during which Durgā is specially worshipped. Nine is also associated with the nine threads (*nava-tāntava*) used in Vedic ritual as well as with a Soma sacrifice with nine Sutyā days (Monier-Williams 1899, p. 531). More generally, there are the nine planets, the nine doors or apertures of the body, nine precious gems (considered related to the nine planets), the nine sentiments in drama, and so on (ibid.). The specific symbolic meaning of this number and the origin of its auspiciousness, however, are not very clear to us.

An important aspect of the multiplicity of the Nine Durgās is their ultimate oneness. The nine goddesses are evidently multiplied manifestations of the one Goddess. They share one or other of the Goddess's aspects, e.g. her fierceness, her power underlying all vegetation, certain events or functions significant in the Goddess's career.

A further aspect of multiplicity of the Nine Durgās is the inverse of this oneness: that is, despite the oneness of Durgā, her tremendous power (whether it be martial power or the power inherent in fertility) appears to the devotee in multiplicity, perhaps, so as to convey its full greatness.

Perhaps, these two aspects—their oneness and multiple manifestations of the one Goddess's power—are to be seen simultaneously, as indicated by their iconographical representations. While depicting all the nine goddesses separately, the iconographical representations clearly distinguish the central, eighteen-armed goddess (who takes the position of the hub of a circle) from the surrounding, peripheral, sixteen-armed goddesses (who are her manifestations).

## 10. THE TEN MAHĀVIDYĀS

### 10.1 GENERAL DESCRIPTION

The Mahāvidyās (described in detail in Danielou 1964, pp. 268–84; Kinsley 1986, pp. 161–65; Kumar 1974, pp. 155–60) include some who are individually important (e.g. Kālī) but do form a distinct group which may be considered, as Kinsley says, to be 'a medieval iconographic and mythological expression of an aspect of Mahādevī theology'—viz. 'the Devī's tendency to display or manifest herself in a great variety of forms' (1986, p. 161). The Mahāvidyās also seem to be of great importance in Tantrism as symbols of the ten objects of transcendent knowledge (Danielou 1964, pp. 268ff; Kumar 1974, pp. 155ff). The Ten Mahāvidyās, who are depicted in many goddess temples throughout India, seem to be regarded as expressing the way in which the particular temple's goddess assumes many different forms (Kinsley 1986, p. 161).

In mythology, the Ten Mahāvidyās come into being in the course of the story of Śiva and Satī (*Mahābhāgavata Purāṇa* 8.50–52; summarized by Kinsley 1986, pp. 162–63). When Dakṣa, Satī's father, decided to perform a great sacrifice, he invited everyone residing in the heaven to attend it, except for Śiva and Satī because he did not like Śiva's uncivilized habits and appearance. Satī, greatly insulted (though Śiva was not), intended to go to disrupt the sacrifice but was forbidden by Śiva to attend the sacrifice. Unable to change her husband's mind, Satī eventually lost her temper, assuming a dreadful form. She then went on to multiply herself into ten different forms, which are Mahāvidyās—Kālī, Tārā, Chinnamastā, Bhuvaneśvarī, Bagalā, Dhūmāvatī, Kamalā, Mātaṅgī, Ṣoḍaśī, and Bhairavī. These ten goddesses are meant to be fearsome, for the story says that the terrible forms that Satī had assumed surrounded and frightened Śiva, so that he gave her permission to attend the sacrifice in return for withdrawing the ten goddesses.

The list of the Ten Mahāvidyās is the same in the *Muṇḍalālā Tantra* (Goudriaan 1981, p. 65), though the goddesses are listed in a different order. Some other lists of Mahāvidyās include goddesses different from the ten given above, besides containing more than ten goddesses (Kinsley 1986, pp. 242–43).

## 10.2 THE FEMALES' RELATIONSHIP WITH MALES

From the above mythological account, it seems clear that, in regard to the Ten Mahāvidyās, the females are considered dominant over the male. Though the source of the ten goddesses (i.e. Satī) is Śiva's wife and appears to be dominated by him (e.g. she needs permission to attend her father's sacrifice), the Ten Mahāvidyās eventually completely surround and frighten Śiva so that Satī could have her own way. In a sense, the ten goddesses show that Satī's real power, which is ordinarily hidden, is greater than Śiva's.

## 10.3 MODE AND AIM OF WORSHIP/OTHER PRACTICE

In metaphysical terms, the Ten Mahāvidyās represent the objects of transcendent knowledge, or various aspects of the source of all that is to be known (Danielou 1964, p. 268). This supreme knowledge, it would appear, is to be gained through the destruction of unwholesome knowledge, and this destruction is what the Ten Mahāvidyās are primarily envisaged as effecting. For the ten goddesses, who are mythologically portrayed as fearsome deities, seem to represent mainly the powers of destruction in the worship of the Ten Mahāvidyās. It is through the destruction of one's ordinary, habitual way of looking at things and through appreciating the power of time, of death, etc., that one is liberated from bondage and comes to live without making life a burden (ibid., p. 268). Such then seems to be one of the primary aims of the worship of these ten goddesses.

## 10.4 MEANING OF MULTIPLICITY

Kumar (1974, p. 155) suggests that the number ten was chosen to match the ten primary incarnations of Viṣṇu. As Kinsley (1986, pp. 162–64) shows, however, the Ten Mahāvidyās are no mere Śākta version of the Vaiṣṇava idea of Viṣṇu's ten *avatāras*. At any rate, one thing that might be suggested for both sets of ten is that the number ten may have been considered potent as the point of completion of one cycle and beginning of a higher cycle. There are, for example, such expressions as *daśa-śata* (=1000) and *daśa-sāhasrika* (=10000). Beyond this, however, we seem unable to discover any intrinsic symbolic value of the number ten.

A significant point regarding the multiplicity found in the Ten Mahāvidyās is that, mythologically, the ten goddesses are not entirely separate or different from one another, they are in fact different forms assumed by one goddess, viz. Satī. Not only does she manifest herself in these ten forms, but she also withdraws them back into herself. As we have noted above, this group of ten goddesses probably represents Mahādevī's tendency to manifest or display herself in a great variety of forms.

PART II

## 11. PLAN OF PART II

In Part I, we have looked at some of the major manifestations of feminine multiplicity in Hinduism (i.e. some of the representative groups of multiple goddesses) *individually* and considered the meanings of feminine multiplicity within the context of each individual group. There are many specific numbers involved in feminine multiplicity (e.g. seven, eight, nine, ten, twelve, sixty-four). Of particular importance to us is the number seven, which, according to our investigation, was regarded by many ancient observers of nature as possessing intrinsic significance, primarily because of the septpartite nature of certain natural phenomena that were significant to them, e.g. the seven colours of the visible spectrum, the visible planets of the solar system, the diatonic musical scale, the lunar cycle (which is a multiple heptad), and the Pleiades. Those ancient people seem to have arranged their world scheme on the basis of seven so as to live in harmony with the rhythms of the universe. We have seen that what is signified by the number seven in that context may be the completion of a cycle and the beginning of a new cycle.

In regard to the other numbers associated with feminine multiplicity, however, we have been unable to uncover deep intrinsic symbolic values, other than the auspiciousness of some of them (many numbers are said to be auspicious in India anyway). Nevertheless, we have come up with some symbolic meanings of multiplicity (if not necessarily connected with specific numbers) involved in groups of female deities.

We may recapitulate these meanings briefly. Clues to understanding the meaning of the multiplicity of the Vedic female heptads, the aboriginal Seven Sisters/Virgins, and the Saptamātṛkās included the intrinsically powerful number seven. In addition, the constellation Kṛttikās indicated the power of yearly renewal; ceremonies held in honour of the Seven Sisters seem to be a means of renewing the order and integrity of the village; and the ceremonial use of oil lamps was indicative of the nature of rites of renewal. The multiplicity of these groups of females, then, seems to have symbolized a cyclic (e.g. yearly) renewal, which means a cyclic return to an original point, which is, again, a new beginning of another unfolding process. The Saptamātṛkās' multiplicity—because of the specific iconographical arrangement of the seven goddesses (particularly, Brahmāṇī, Vaiṣṇavī, and Cāmuṇḍā)—seems also to have represented a spiritual renewal or spiritual return to the original source of all, a spiritual rebirth. In the case of the letters (*mātṛkās*), which involved the numbers eight (the number of the classes of the letters) and fifty, their multiplicity seems, through their linguistic cosmology and ontology, to indicate the power, both, to bring about great diversity that constitutes the entire manifest cosmos and to affirm this diversity's essential identity with the *one* universal source of everything. The Sixty-four Yoginīs' multiplicity seems also to be connected with the letters' meaning of multiplicity since, at least in a certain tradition, these goddesses are explicitly derived in eight groups from the eight presiding Mothers of the eight classes of the Sanskrit letters and since, in some other traditions, the number sixty-four is clearly understood as the square of eight, a number indicative of the letters' eight class goddesses. Further, the worship of the Yoginīs in the form of a circle and, particularly, their diagrammatic representation such as found in the Khecarī Cakra point to the notion of the unfolding of the multiple Yoginīs from the primordial unity-centre and the return of the multiples back to the original source. The multiplicity of the Śrī-Cakra's deities expresses a variety of powers of Śakti, which, on the one hand, enable essential Consciousness to bring itself into manifold forms and, on the other, return the manifold to the One. The wheel of the Twelve Kālīs accounts for the emanation and withdrawal of essential cosmic Consciousness from and back into itself. Moreover, this wheel affirms the fundamental, perfect identity of manifestations and their source. The Nine Durgās express their ultimate oneness and the greatness of Durgā's power, which manifests the Goddess in multiple forms. The Ten Mahāvidyās' multiplicity is connected with the Devī's power to take various forms and to withdraw them.

What conclusion is to be drawn from all this? This synopsis indicates that our discussions have yielded two main ideas regarding the meaning of feminine multiplicity: (1) renewal (cyclic or spiritual), or a return to an original point, which is a new beginning of another unfolding process, and (2) the emanation of the One as the manifold and the withdrawal of the manifold back into the One, so to speak. These two ideas, further, both recognize the process of *unfolding* from an Origin and the reverse process of *return* to the Origin. This—the process of successive *unfolding* and *return* from and back to the Origin—then, is what we have come up with in our attempt to discover the meaning of feminine multiplicity.

Yet, we have by no means exhausted the meaning of feminine multiplicity of Hinduism, for there are many questions that have not been answered. For instance, though we have discussed the inherent value of the number seven in regard to the Seven Sisters/ Virgins (as well as the Saptamātṛkās, etc., for that matter), the number seven for the aboriginal/Dravidian Sisters is actually not always consistent. Examples of eight, nine, thirteen or more sisters or goddesses as a group are known (Crooke 1896, p. 112; Whitehead 1921, p. 232; cf. Kosambi 1962, p. 86). How do we explain these groupings? Further, if we accept the astronomical explanation of the intrinsic power of the number seven, how do we account for the fact that, even after the astronomical association of the number seven ceased as a physically observable fact (the alignment of the Pleiades and the vernal equinox last occurred in 1730 BCE—Harper 1977, p. 82), the worship of the Saptamātṛkās, the Seven Sisters/Virgins, etc. still flourished? Again, given the evidently numerous groups of females, and given that some groups are tremendously large (e.g. the innumerable Mātṛs in the ch. 46 of the *Śalya Parva* of the Mbh), why is it the *feminine*, not the *masculine*, that multiplies so extensively? How do we account for the following ambivalence of the Saptamātṛkās: the discrepancy between the benign maternity of icons of the Saptamātṛkās and the inimical mothers of epic-Purāṇic literature, on the one hand, and between the iconographical representations of the six *deva-śaktis* (who are mild) and the *devī-śakti*, Cāmuṇḍā (who is fierce), on the other?

Could it be that clues to answering these questions are to be found in certain, particularly Indian ways of perceiving women? My hypothesis underlying Part II of this study is that there are connections between the prominence of feminine multiplicity in India and the Indian perception of women. Much of Part II is concerned with examining two kinds of explanation of feminine multiplicity based upon this hypothesis. One kind of explanation is connected with a demeaning perception of women, which is the officially sanctioned perception of women in the Brahmanical tradition. This ex planation links feminine multiplicity with male chauvinism that says that women are all the same, that women cannot do anything alone, that several women are required to equal one man, and so forth. The other kind of explanation is derived from the perception of women as powerful and complex beings—a perception that is not officially admitted but is still discernible in mythology and folklore, among other things. From this second perspective, one might explain that the complexity and power of the feminine is so great that she needs to be seen in multiplicity to represent her full implications. In short, one image is not enough.

## 12. IS FEMININE MULTIPLICITY DEMEANING?

In this chapter, I shall examine the first of the above-mentioned two kinds of explanation of feminine multiplicity, viz. that a demeaning perception of women arising from male chauvinism underlies feminine multiplicity. This kind of perception of women is very much borne out by the *Laws of Manu*, the most authoritative of the Hindu law-books representing the official Brahmanical values. The *Laws of Manu* sets forth an evidently male-dominated world-view (the following translation of all passages quoted from this book is by Bühler 1886):

> Him to whom her father may give her, or her brother with the father's permission, she shall obey as long as he lives, and when he is dead, she must not insult (his memory).
>
> … the betrothal (by the father or guardian) is the cause of (the husband's) dominion (over his wife) (5.151–52).
>
> Though destitute of virtue, or seeking pleasure (elsewhere), or devoid of good qualities, (yet) a husband must be constantly worshipped as a god by a faithful wife (5.154).
>
> A faithful wife, who desires to dwell (after death) with her husband, must never do anything that might displease him who took her hand, whether he be alive or dead (5.156).
>
> … a woman who from a desire to have offspring violates

> her duty towards her (deceased) husband, brings on herself disgrace in this world, and loses her place with husband (in heaven) (5.161).

Thus, women are instructed to demonstrate absolute obedience and faithfulness to their husbands. This male-dominated world-view involves the idea that women are utterly incapable of doing anything independently:

> By a girl, by a young woman, or even by an aged one, nothing must be done independently, even in her own house.
>
> In childhood a female must be subject to her father, in youth to her husband, when her lord is dead to her sons; a woman must never be independent (5.147–48).
>
> No sacrifice, no vow, no fast must be performed by women apart (from their husband); if a wife obeys her husband, she will for that (reason alone) be exalted in heaven (5.155).
>
> Day and night women must be kept in dependence by the males (of) their (families), and, if they attach themselves to sensual enjoyments, they must be kept under one's control.
>
> Her father protects (her) in childhood, her husband protects (her) in youth, and her sons protect (her) in old age; a

woman is never fit for independence (9.2–3).

Such a perception of women can easily be imagined as giving rise to male chauvinism that says that women cannot do anything alone, that all women are the same, and that several women are required to match one man. Could it be, then, that this kind of demeaning perception of women has led to the formation of the concept of groups of multiple goddesses? An indication that this kind of perception might be linked to groups of multiple mother-goddesses is found in the following verse of Manu: 'If among all the wives of one husband one has a son, Manu declares them all (to be) mothers of male children through that son' (9.183).

Some groups of female deities might, indeed, appear to be explained by this interpretation. The Saptamātṛkās are usually housed in Śiva temples and are described by Kramrisch (1975, p. 263) as being under the leadership of Śiva. This interpretation, however, is not free of all problems. First, the seven goddesses are not wives of Śiva. Second, six of them are the energies of male deities who, as we have seen, cannot function without them. Third, the seventh is the energy of no male deity; she is a *devī-śakti*. Fourth, mythological accounts indicate that the seven goddesses' primary roles are to accomplish a task for male deities, who cannot fulfil it themselves.

The leader of the Sixty-four Yoginīs is also said to be Śiva (Dehejia 1986, p. 35). For one thing, however, the Sixty-four Yoginīs are not all the same; they have quite strong individual characters, though most of them do have in common a chthonic nature (ibid., pp. 194–216). Further, in the Yoginī Kula tradition, Bhairava was to be equated with the practitioner's own inner transcendent identity, which then was to be fused, in intense, mystical experience, with the Yoginīs, who have to be gratified through specific offerings (Sanderson 1988, p. 680). From such a mystical perspective, the supposed male chauvinism on the part of Bhairava is irrelevant to this male-female relationship. If anything, it is the Yoginīs who dominate this relationship, for Bhairava is identified with the human worshipper whereas the females are considered divine. In the cases of both the Saptamātṛkās and the Sixty-four Yoginīs, then, the males seem to have no substantial role or power—certainly no superiority over the females.

There are some instances of male dominance. In the Mbh, 'all the Mothers of the world' approached Skanda but, when they saw him, they realized that 'he was invincible [and thus] they sought refuge with him' (3.215.15ff; tr. van Buitenen 1975, p. 652). But, of course, these Mothers were evidently considered to be more powerful than any other male and, hence, had been asked by the gods to kill Skanda, to begin with. Another instance of male dominance involving feminine multiplicity may be found in a later episode from the same text where the seven sages' six wives beseech Skanda to save them from the unjust allegation of their unfaithfulness to their husbands (Mbh 3.219.1ff).

On the whole, however, is the demeaning perception of women a satisfactory account of feminine multiplicity? I think not. In fact, there are, even, clear counter-examples to show the unsatisfactoriness of this explanation. For instance, we read in the Mbh:

> Devī created Brahmā, Viṣṇu, and Śiva. Then she divided herself into three parts and promised to become the wife of each of them. She instructed them to create, preserve, and destroy the universe, and she promised to bear them

all children (3.15ff; tr. O'Flaherty 1980, p. 98)

Not only is the general flavour of female dominance very clear, but three separate males are there to match three forms of a single Goddess. Though this story goes on to say that Śiva tries to obtain the Devī for his wife alone, and succeeds in doing so, all the three gods are tested by this one Goddess in the selection process. Śiva, then, further, woos the Devī with asceticism and *bhakti*. Here, then, we have a situation that is the exact opposite of male chauvinism. So much for the idea that feminine multiplicity is demeaning.

# 13. PERCEPTION OF WOMEN AS POWERFUL AND COMPLEX BEINGS—LITERARY EVIDENCE

In chapters 13 to 15, I shall consider the second of the aforementined two kinds of explanation of feminine multiplicity. This explanation says that women are perceived in India as powerful and complex beings and that the power and complexity of the feminine are so great that the feminine has to be seen in multiplicity to represent her full implications. In Part I, in fact, sections entitled 'The Females' Relationship with Males' have already indicated that most of the groups of females that we have considered involve some form or other of acknowledgement of the greatness of feminine power in contrast to the relative powerlessness of the males. In short, such groups of multiple females involve female dominance in the male-female power relationship. In the course of the next three chapters, I shall look at feminine power and complexity in more detail. To begin with, chapter 13 will present literary evidence—taken from the Vedas, the *Laws of Manu*, and post-Vedic material—for the Indian perception of women as complex and powerful beings. Chapter 14 will give anthropological, psychoanalytical, and folklore-related evidence for this perception of women. Chapter 15 will, then, produce supporting material for the idea that the power and complexity of the feminine actually results in her *splitting* and *multiplying*.

## 13.1 FROM VEDIC LITERATURE

We have seen earlier that the Waters (identified with the Seven Mothers) are the givers of the life force (RV 10.9.1), or the power underlying life in general. They have the power to ensure the well-being and health of people, and they are the healing power itself (RV 10.9.4–7, 10.97). They even have the power to dispel evils that men have committed (RV 10.9.8). Aditi, personified as a goddess, is also a prime example of the power to give life. She is described literally as crouching with legs spread to give birth to space itself, the earth, and the gods of the sky (RV 10.72).

The Vedic perception of the feminine power, however, is not always straightforward. While Dawn and Night are also seen as sources of the power of life as well as praised as beautiful women, it is said that Dawn was a woman who intended to do evil and was eventually slain by Indra (RV 4.30.8–11). The danger of the power of the feminine—which makes feminine power complex—is also seen in the remark made by Urvaśī (herself portrayed as 'immoral, dangerous, and cruel' (O'Flaherty 1980, p. 79)):

> Women have the hearts of hyenas (RV 10.95.15; tr. O'Flaherty ibid.).

The danger of feminine power is also evident at RV 1.179.4, which reads, 'The foolish woman sucks dry the panting wise man' (tr. ibid.).

## 13.2 FROM THE *LAWS OF MANU*

In chapter 12 above, we noted that this authoritative law-book sets forth an extremely male-dominated world-view, which must have been instrumental in giving rise to the official Hindu demeaning perception of women. Even in this law-book, however, we have evidence for the Hindus' officially unadmitted perception of women as powerful beings who are *not at all straightforward or simple or easy to handle*. For instance, the dangerous power of women to seduce men is very much recognized. We read:

> It is the nature of women to seduce men in this (world); for that reason the wise are never unguarded in (the company of) females.
>
> For women are *able* to lead astray in (this) world not only a fool, but even a learned man, and (to make) him a slave of desire and anger (my italics).
>
> One should not sit in a lonely place with one's mother, sister, or daughter; for the senses are powerful, and master even a learned man (2.213–15).

In the *Laws of Manu*, feminine power is not restricted to seduction. Sometimes the nature of feminine power is not clearly defined, and the text gives the impression that this power is more all-encompassing. The text says for instance that the power of the feminine is so tremendous that it can cause great trouble if women are displeased.

> Where women are honoured, there the gods are pleased; but where they are not honoured, no sacred rite yields rewards (3.57).

Thus, feminine power can even annul the efficacy of sacred rites. The power of displeased women can be extremely dangerous.

> The houses on which female relations, not being duly honoured, pronounce a curse, perish completely, as if destroyed by magic (5.58).

Very often, feminine power is seen as derived from the biological structure of the female body. We have already noted the feminine power to seduce men. But there are many more aspects to the power that is based on the female body. For instance, it is in the female body that the power to conceive a child is found. Thus, Manu says:

> … if the wife is not radiant with beauty, she will not attract her husband; but if she has no attractions for him, no children will be born (3.61).

Further, while all bodily fluids are considered impure in the Hindu tradition in general, the menstrual blood is regarded as one of the most impure substances. It is extremely potent—its power to pollute is tremendous. Thus, great attention is paid by Manu to how one should avoid falling victim to this aspect of feminine power.

> Let him [Snātaka (=Brāhmaṇa who has completed his studentship)], though mad with desire, not approach his wife when her courses appear; nor let him sleep with her in the same bed.

> For the wisdom, the energy, the strength, the sight, and the vitality of a man who approaches a woman covered with menstrual excretions, utterly perish.

> ... Let him not converse with a menstruating woman....
>
> Let him never eat (food ...) ... touched by a menstruating woman ... (4.40–41, 57, 207–08).

Also greatly feared as dangerous is the birth blood and the birth-related power to pollute, which remains potent for a certain period of time following childbirth:

> [Let him never eat food] prepared for a woman in childbed ... nor that (given by a woman) whose ten days of impurity have not elapsed (4.212).

Lastly, female power is summed up as follows by Manu:

> The female relatives (have power) over the world of the Apsarases, the maternal relatives over that of the Viśve Devās, the connexions by marriage over that of the waters, the mothers and the maternal uncle over the earth (4.183).

## 13.3 FROM POST-VEDIC LITERATURE

In the literature of the post-Vedic period, the Hindu perception of women as powerful and complex beings is even more openly expressed. I shall give examples of the supporting material for this below, but essentially, what this material says seems to be that the feminine is extremely powerful and her power is complicated because it is both good (e.g. life-producing) and bad (e.g. dangerous, destructive). One way to look at how this perception of women as powerful and complex beings may have arisen has been suggested by O'Flaherty:

> She [the woman] has two sites of sexual fluids to his [the man's] one, and the one that they share (the genital site) is doubly productive in her (of both seed and blood). Moreover, the fluid that they share—blood—is also ambiguous in her: her blood is in part productive but life-draining (venous blood, producing milk and female seed) and in part dangerous but life-creating (menstrual blood, acting as female seed). Her milk, issuing from her secondary sexual site, is similarly ambivalent. ... The symbolism of ambivalent milk is enhanced by the belief that, since milk is good, an evil woman has either no milk or else poison in her breasts, like Pūtanā [who tries to kill the infant Kṛṣṇa by poison-smeared breasts—*Bhāgavata Purāṇa* 10.6.1ff] (O'Flaherty 1980, pp. 53–54; material within brackets supplied).

This certainly seems to be a useful way of interpreting how feminine power and complexity might arise, but we do not have to conform to the details contained in this interpretation all the time. What is important for our purposes is that the feminine does seem to be perceived as powerful and that her power is seen as complicated because it can be both good and bad.

In the Mbh, for instance, we have looked at the Mothers of the world, who were dispatched to kill Skanda. Upon seeing him, they not only realized his invincible strength but, more importantly here, they were also overcome by their maternal instinct, thus producing milk for him and eventually guarding him as their son. The Mothers say to him: 'You are our son. We hold the world. Welcome us all, we are yielding milk, overcome with love' (Mbh 3.215.15ff; tr. van Buitenen 1975, p. 652). Here, we see some ambivalence involved in the Mothers' maternal love, for they were originally intending to kill the infant Skanda and later gave in to their maternal power, which enabled them to yield milk for him and guard him. Further, in a later passage (Mbh 3.219.13ff; tr. van Buitenen 1975, pp. 657ff), there are indications that their maternal power could be misguided and become the cause of danger to children. After another group of mothers became the Mothers of all the world as well as the 'seven mothers of newborn sons' by the grace of Skanda, the original Mothers of the world say to Skanda, 'They [the second group of mothers] have robbed our progeny on your account, restore it to us!' But Skanda replies: 'You cannot cherish progeny that have been given away. I'll bestow on you what other offspring you may desire.' Then, the original Mothers say, 'We want to devour the offspring of those Mothers—give them to us....' To this, Skanda, though telling them to spare the offspring when they honour them well, allows them to afflict the young children of men in their various forms until they are sixteen years of age. The Mothers are then described as horrible Graspers, who afflict, snatch, or eat children and foetuses. This story, then, may be seen as an instance of maternal power that is perceived both as capable of deep love for children and as potentially dangerous to children.

In the Purāṇas, there are many instances of feminine power portrayed as great and as ambivalent (both good and dangerous). We shall look at some examples that are representative of the ways in which the texts describe feminine power and complexity.

First, the DM, which marks the first emergence of the Goddess as the central deity, describes her as being created through uniting the key powers of the most powerful of the male deities (DM ch. 2). This story shows that her power is superior to that of any male deity (and to that of anyone for that matter). Her great power is portrayed as good, as far as her primary role in the story is concerned, for she is created expressly to defeat the demons harmful to the world. Her power is not without complexity, however, for the chthonic nature of her power is fully evident from the way she kills the demons. For instance, she kills Raktabīja by drinking all his blood (DM 8.52ff). We might also say—from the point of view of the masculine—that the dangerous nature of her power is implicit in the fact that it is *male* demons that she kills. Further, there are some indications that Mahiṣa, the buffalo demon to be killed, is actually her husband (e.g. O'Flaherty 1980, p. 81; Onishi 1995). Her dangerousness is further indicated by the superiority that she enjoys over the male gods: She can fulfil a role that no male deity can (viz. defeating the demon enemies of the world). This female dominance runs counter to the officially sanctioned position of women which we mentioned earlier.

Many instances of female dominance in the Purāṇas, with special reference to the various versions of the Mahiṣa myth (which is the archetypal myth of the goddess in India (Shulman 1980, p. 177)), have been documented by O'Flaherty (1980, pp. 80ff). We shall note just a few more examples here. For instance, some Tamil texts explicitly portray the Goddess as killing her buffalo consort by cutting off his head, which is identifiable with his phallus (ibid., pp. 81, 84). If the identification of the buffalo demon as the Goddess's consort is not clear in the Sanskrit Purāṇas, their erotic relationship at least is often discernible enough. Here again, this relationship can be characterized by female sexual supremacy and (from the point of view of the males) sexual danger. For instance, a variant of the Mahiṣa myth describes the Goddess as threatening to engage him in aggressive love play in the 'inverted' position and to drain him of his semen, i.e. his life's breath (cited in ibid., p. 83). Thus, it would appear that, through the Mahiṣa myths, the Purāṇas portray the feminine as aggressive, castrating, and dangerous.

A good example of feminine power and complexity as perceived and expressed in the Purāṇas is found in the *Matsya Purāṇa* account—which we looked at briefly earlier—of the gods' battle against the demon Andhaka (179.8–90, summarized by Kinsley 1986, pp. 158–59; similar accounts also in *Vāmana Purāṇa* 43 & *Viṣṇudharmottara Purāṇa* 1.226.1–82, as noted in O'Flaherty 1973, pp. 280–81). There, the Mātṛkās are said to defeat Andhaka for Śiva by devouring this demon and others who arise from each drop of Andhaka's blood. Following the battle, however, the Mātṛkās proceed to devour the gods and people and had to be stopped by another band of goddesses. The power of the feminine here fulfils the roles that the males could not fulfil—viz. not only devouring the demons, but also suppressing the misguided female power which has gone overboard. What makes this feminine power complicated is the great danger that this very power is capable of bringing, i.e. devouring even the gods and people.

From time to time, the complicated power of the feminine is manifested in the Purāṇas as a wife's power to refuse her husband intercourse. Sometimes, this power is employed to keep her husband faithful to her. For instance, a myth in a Tamil Śaiva text reads:

> A certain potter once violated his marriage vows by making

> love to a dancing girl. His wife made him swear by the name of Śiva that he would never touch any woman, not even her ... (quoted in O'Flaherty 1973, p. 61).

In myths dealing with a woman's refusal of sex, however, the man may not always be forbidden to have casual sexual relations though he is prohibited from making love to his wife (or a woman he loves) (O'Flaherty 1980, p. 57). The point seems to be that feminine power forbids the man to have intercourse with the most auspicious partner. This means that the female's refusal of sex is inauspicious.

One important feature of goddess myths contained in the Tamil texts, as shown by Shulman (1980, e.g. pp. 349–50), is that, after puberty, a virgin is regarded as a locus of power, sealed within limits and preserved from physical contact. Her complexity is that, though she is an epitome of purity, she is also seen as exploding with 'pent-up erotic power' and as a symbol of the seductive, menacing force. The danger remains latent as long as this force is shut up and contained. If, however, a male comes into contact with her, he lets loose the great force of the virgin's power *against himself*.

When we turn to descriptions of Tantric ritual, we find that supernatural power and deeply chthonic features are attributed to females, such as Ḍākinīs. The Ḍākinīs are said to have the ability to fly in the air, but initiation into their fold involves the eating of human flesh (Dehejia 1986, p. 15). They are also very fond of '(ritual) menstrual blood and "the seed of bodily conception"' (O'Flaherty 1980, p. 237). Queen Kuvalayavatī, for instance, is described as a Ḍākinī in the *Kathāsaritsāgara*. Upon returning from an expedition unexpectedly, her king finds her

> stark naked, with her hair standing on end and her lips trembling in muttering charms, in the midst of a great circle (*mahāmaṇḍala-madhyagām*) strewed with various coloured powders, after offering a horrible oblation of blood, spirits and human flesh (quoted in Dehejia 1986, p. 16).

The queen then confesses to being a Ḍākinī and relates how she was initiated:

> She [the chief Ḍākinī] made me take off my clothes ... and ... she gave me various spells known to her, and human flesh to eat.... After I had eaten man's flesh and had received the various spells, I immediately flew up.... Thus, even in my girlhood I became one of the society of witches (*ḍākinīcakra*), and in our meetings we devoured the bodies of many men (ibid.).

In regard to Tantric cosmology, it is worth noting that the Āgamic cosmic hierarchies seem to be populated by predominantly female, dangerous forces (Sanderson 1988). A prime example is the terrible, castrating Vīrya-Kālī, who rides on Kālāgnirudra's shoulders and who holds a severed head, a sword, a skull-cup, a bleeding heart, and so on (ibid., pp. 675–76). The power and complexity of the feminine is here heightened by the doubly heterodox combination of the castrating feminine and such pollutant materials as blood. The Tantric reversal of the orthodox patterns of male dominance is also exemplified by the Yoginīs, who, as we saw earlier, threaten to become angry with practitioners who insult any women.

Before closing this section, we may note that the emergence of chthonic aspects of feminine power can sometimes be accounted for by unjust mistreatment suffered by the female(s)—a theme which we mentioned in chapter 3 above. For instance, the original 'Mothers of the world' of the Mbh, though chthonic enough to be willing to kill Skanda initially, become even more dangerous and announce their wish to devour children *after* they were robbed of their progeny. Such child-afflicting goddesses may be related to the belief that women who die in childbirth or without a child become inimical spirits who, jealous of other fortunate women and their children, steal or harm the children (Brubaker 1978, pp. 30–31). We have also noted a myth about a potter's wife who refused sex because of her husband's unfaithfulness. Thus, some instances of feminine power and complexity may be explained by the notion of injustice suffered by females. This notion, however, does not by any means apply to all instances, and often no specific explanation seems to be discernible in literary material.

In chapter 13, we have been looking at literary material—taken from the Vedas, the *Laws of Manu*, and post-Vedic literature—that points to the Hindu perception of women as powerful and complex beings. In the next chapter, I shall try to present anthropological, psychoanalytical, and folklore-related evidence for this kind of perception of women. We shall see that such evidence sheds further light on how this particular perception may have originated.

# 14. PERCEPTION OF WOMEN AS POWERFUL AND COMPLEX BEINGS—ANTHROPOLOGICAL, PSYCHOANALYTICAL, AND FOLKLORE-RELATED EVIDENCE

In this chapter, I shall be looking to primarily non-literary material for indications that women are perceived in India as powerful and complex beings. I shall consider this material under four headings: Indus Valley Civilization, aboriginal/Dravidian perception of women, Brahmanical perception of tribal women, and general Brahmanical perception of women.

## 14.1 INDUS VALLEY CIVILIZATION

Hundreds of female figurines—in contrast to only a few male figures—have been found in the sites of the Indus Valley Civilization. This fact suggests that goddesses may have been widely worshipped and exalted in this culture. Hypothesizing that they really were, for the sake of argument, we might attempt to find out the reason for the exalted position of the feminine.

Much of the information we have about the Indus culture's perception of women comes from the seals. The following seals are particularly important to us. One seal shows a nude figure, probably a woman, upside down with her legs spread[6] and a plant emerging from her womb (Banerjea 1956, p. 489). The reverse of this seal depicts a female figure kneeling or seated and male figure standing beside her with what appears to be a sickle (Kinsley 1986, p. 215).

---

[6] We noted the Vedic equivalent to this figure in section 13.1. The RV hymn 10.72 describes Aditi as crouching with legs spread to give birth to space, the earth, and the gods of the sky.

Another seal—we have considered this one in some detail in chapter 1—shows a goddess standing in a pipal (fig tree) and a kneeling figure beside it and an animal facing the goddess. The head of the goddess seems to be adorned by three horns, two of which form a definite crescent shape or the shape of bull horns. The goddess's horns may be linked to creative and fecund powers since the fast-growing horns and the waxing aspect of the moon often indicate the power of invigoration (Harper 1977, p. 12). The association of the bull's horns and regenerative power may be further reinforced by the Old European identity of the bull's head with uterus and regenerative waters (Gimbutas 1989, pp. 265ff with Fig. 411). A third seal shows a nude female figure having an animal head (or mask) who leans over a rearing horned animal. There is a tree beside the female figure, whose hand is placed on the animal's shoulder (Kinsley 1986, p. 215).

Based on the first and second seals, we may say that the Indus culture probably knew a goddess associated with the power underlying vegetation and the fertility of crops. Further, the second and third seals indicate that the Indus people may have associated a goddess with the power of fertility of animals. In sum, then, it is probable that the power underlying vegetation and the fertility of crops and of animals was linked to the feminine in the Indus culture. All this points to a fairly uncomplicated recognition of the power of the feminine. If, however, the second seal is interpreted as depicting a sacrifice scene, as suggested by some scholars (see chapter 1), then this female power is tinged with a chthonic flavour.

## 14.2 ABORIGINAL/DRAVIDIAN PERCEPTION OF WOMEN

Our material relevant to this section seems to indicate that women are identified in this culture with various kinds of powers, many of which connote a chthonic nature. Let us briefly look at some examples.

Among the Agaria tribe, the power of fire, so vital to the transition from the wilderness to civilization, is closely associated with the feminine. In Agaria myths, it is a virgin who showed a sage how to make a fire originally (O'Flaherty 1973, p. 92). Further, as noted by Elwin (cited in ibid.), this power to bring a fire into the world is also deeply linked to the power of sexual attraction of the feminine because of the analogy between the sexual act and the action of the fire-stick and the fire-drill. The sage in the myths, too, gives up his asceticism after seeing the fire.

The sexual power of the feminine is perceived as having some dangerous consequences. For instance, since birth is regarded as polluting, women in childbirth or during a certain length of time after childbirth are believed by the Santals to be capable of cancelling the care provided by good national *bongas* (spirits) (Archer 1974, p. 31). Among the Santals, the danger of feminine sexual power is also expressed by some of the terms used to refer to the vagina, such as 'the scorpion hole', 'the hollow where men fall', and 'the buried *bongas*' (ibid., p. 40). The last term refers to dangerous *bongas*. *Bongas*, some good and others bad, are powerful spirits who are involved in everything that concerns the Santals, who therefore must come to terms with them if they are to live happily (ibid., pp. 26–27). Some are clearly regarded as female, e.g. Rongo Ruji *bonga* (regarded as a female obsessed with sex) and the *bonga* of the house (regarded as quick to take offense, like a touchy, 'testy' woman, and apt to cause disease) (ibid., p. 27).

Feminine power is also regarded as capable of castrating males.

As we have noted earlier, the standard practice, during the buffalo sacrifice, of cutting the animal's foreleg and placing it in its mouth is probably related to a myth about a Brahmin woman beheading her consort, cutting off his penis, and putting it in his mouth (Beck 1981, p. 122n63; O'Flaherty 1980, p. 83).

On the level of South Indian village goddess worship, the ambivalent and complicated nature of feminine power has been demonstrated by Brubaker (1978; also 1979, pp. 129–31). Village goddesses are normally understood as providing protection against threats to the village, typically, epidemic disease, and, when the disease demons do penetrate, the goddesses' power is said to ensure their eventual expulsion. Yet, the epidemic is also regarded as caused by the goddesses' power of anger as a punishment to their people. Again, the disease may also be interpreted as the manifestation of goddesses themselves. Further, the goddesses could themselves be understood as victims of the disease. The linkage of village goddesses with threats to the village seems to be very complex indeed.

In certain tribal societies, women seem to be regarded as potential witches possessing the power to kill or harm people. That is why, among the Santals, a woman is not allowed to say, 'I will eye you' (which it is permissible for a man to say)—she would be fined (Archer 1974, p. 52). Archer records a myth about the origin of witchcraft in which this art of evil powers is ascribed to tensions between the sexes in the family (ibid., pp. 292–93). The myth tells of how women, upon finding out that their husbands are learning an art of making women respect men, got the better of men by learning the incantations and the art of eating men. The Santals seem to believe that the female power to become a witch arises at puberty. A witch's training as believed among the Santals has been described by Archer (ibid., pp. 298–94). Archer says that, generally, an old woman lures a girl into learning the art of witchcraft by telling her about the powers that the art confers and about other fellow witches. When she consents to listen, the old witch begins singing the witches' songs. Once the girl hears such songs, however, she is to become a witch or die. Now the requirements that she must fulfil to qualify for full membership include learning the art of killing from a *bonga* and eating onc of her own family members. The power of the evil eye is believed in also by the Mundas, who, in times of repeated sickness in a family or among cattle, appeal to a witch-finder for detecting the responsible witch (Roy 1970, p. 279). 'In times within living memory, people accused of witchcraft but denying the charge have sometimes been beaten to death' (ibid.).

In tribal societies especially, but by no means exclusively, women seem to be regarded as imbued with mysterious, strange powers. For instance, a tribe in Orissa, known as the Gadaba, possesses a myth (considered in chapter 3) that ascribes the origin of toddy—representing the power of intoxication—to seven sisters. Also, Santal girls are not allowed, e.g., to climb a roof because they can pollute the *bongas*, who would then stop rain (Archer 1974, p. 53). For the same reason, girls must avoid a number of other acts, e.g. going near the trunks of trees in the sacred grove (ibid., p. 292). The Santal girls could also stop rain by ploughing a field. Santal widows are also sometimes considered capable of harming people, and in a festival held in July, the priest prays to the good *bongas* for protection against them (ibid., p. 30).

It seems clear from the foregoing that, in aboriginal/Dravidian culture, women are perceived as possessing strong powers which are complex and multivalent.

## 14.3 BRAHMANICAL PERCEPTION OF TRIBAL WOMEN

As suggested by Goudriaan (1979, p. 31), it may have been Tantric practitioners with a tendency to wander or settle away from the centres of Hindu culture that were most likely to come 'into contact, not only with the common people of Hinduized areas, but also with non-Hindu peoples and tribes who worshipped strange deities and practised deviating religious customs'. One of the clearest indications of the Hindus' contacts with tribes is supplied by the *Harivaṃśa*, which contains a hymn to Āpyā (Durgā) in which she is portrayed as the goddess of such wild tribes as Śabaras, Pulindas, and Barbaras and as fond of wine and flesh (Bhandarkar 1913, p. 143).

Let us look at tribal women's features that must have been most striking to the Hindus. For instance, the Naga women all smoke pipes (Elwin 1969, p. 68), eat animals of all kinds, including rats, snakes, monkeys; tigers, and elephants (ibid., p. 101–02), and drink rice beer in great quantities (bid., p. 102). They would drink anything, but apparently, the stronger it is, the better (ibid., p. 626). It is of course both sexes, not just women, that do smoking, flesh-eating, and drinking. But, to the Hindus—whose idea of how women should behave was characterized by such qualities as being subordinate, modest, etc.—tribal women must have looked extremely powerful and even overwhelming. These descriptions of women seem to apply also to Munda women as reported by Roy (1970, pp. 218–311).

## 14.4 GENERAL BRAHMANICAL PERCEPTION OF WOMEN

The point here is that the power and complexity of the feminine is indicated by two contrasting images of the feminine—one representing the conscious Hindu ideal of wifely virtues, such as purity, beauty, fidelity, benevolence, and softness, and the other reflecting a secret conviction among many Hindu men that the feminine principle is really the opposite, terrible, treacherous, unpredictable, vengeful, and rampant with insatiable, contaminating sexuality (Kakar 1978, p. 93; Carstairs 1957, pp. 156–57). According to psychoanalytical and anthropological evidence, this two-sided complex perception of powerful women seems to originate in early childhood and results largely from the role of women as prescribed in Brahmanical values. To explain the Brahmanical perception of women as complex and powerful beings, the following causal nexus, suggested by Obeyesekere, seems useful:

> The values of the society —› the female role —› mother-child relationship —› perception of the deity by the child (Obeyesekere 1984, p. 429).

The last element in the nexus says 'perception of the deity ...' because Obeyesekere is essentially trying to explain contrasting images of the Hindu mother-goddess (e.g. Pārvatī and Kālī). For our purposes, however, we can replace 'the deity' with 'women'. Below, I recapitulate relevant parts of Obeyesekere's explanation (ibid., pp. 427–443) while supplying further information from other sources where appropriate.

Brahmanical values teach that goals of marriage are *dharma* (religious duty), *prajā* (progeny), and *rati* (pleasure)—thus, sex is of least importance. The female ideal is wifely devotion, and its concomitants are virginity at marriage, and faithfulness, unassertiveness, submissiveness, and unquestioning loyalty to the husband. The woman must treat her husband as a god (relevant Manu passages have been quoted in chapter 12 above). The suppression of the woman's sex and aggressive drives begins, in fact, long before marriage since the role of women is taught from early childhood. The woman's suppression is made worse by such factors as: early (generally, child) marriage resulting from preoccupation with virginity at marriage; patrilocal marital residence; the need for the girl to adjust to the roles of the wife and daughter-in-law under the harsh regime of the mother-in-law; the wife's unsatisfied need for love due to her husband's aloofness mainly because of arranged marriage and the joint family setting; and so forth.

The only release, then, is her relationship with her children. The wife develops an intense symbiotic attachment to her son especially because she had the great fear, until his birth, of not having a male heir, who is indispensable for performing funeral ritual that will ensure the father's salvation and who will also look after her when he grows up. The whole life of the woman is centred on her first son. Such maternal attitudes to the son promote the child's fixation on her as a good, loving mother.

This relationship, however, has another dimension. Since the woman is sexually repressed, some of her sexual longings receive expression in the daily intimacy of her contact with her son, the mother being a kind of seductress of the child. For instance, the mother may unself-consciously kiss the son's penis. According to Kakar, clinical experience has demonstrated that

> the displacement of a woman's sexual longings from her husband to her son poses one of the most difficult problems for a boy to handle.... [The] mother's touch and stimulation ... arouse an intensity of feeling in the male child

> which his still weak and unstructured ego cannot cope with. ... [A]lthough he unconditionally needs the physical tending and emotional sustenance that at first only his mother provides, he is profoundly afraid of being overwhelmed and 'devoured' by her. As the infant boy grows ..., he senses that he cannot do without his mother nor remove himself from her presence, but at the same time he is incapable of giving her what she unconsciously desires. 'Realizing' his inadequacy in this regard, he also begins to fear his mother's anger.... In his fantasy, the mother's body and especially her genitals may assume an ominous aspect (1978, p. 91).

Thus seems to arise the image of a mother who sexually assaults her son.

The perception of the mother as a terrible, powerful, and frightening being seems also attributable to the shock that weaning brings to the child who is deeply attached to the mother. The child is never separated from the mother for long during their first year (Carstairs 1957, p. 157). The infant is never allowed to cry long (Kakar 1978, p. 81) and, whenever hungry or distressed or upset, is given the breast generously (Carstairs 1957, p. 157) or else picked up, rocked, or otherwise comforted (Kakar 1978, p. 80). The mother is the infant's willing slave, and the child seems to experience very little frustration during the pre-weaning period (Carstairs 1957, p. 157). The child is weaned late in India—even as late as his third or fourth year—when he is becoming increasingly conscious of occurrences in his life, including the familiar protection and nurturing provided by his mother and physically represented by her breasts (Kakar 1978, p. 147). He will also have noticed that the mother is sometimes aloof in the presence of her parents-in-law and that at night his father often claims his mother, whom the child has monopolized before (Carstairs 1957, p. 157). The feeling of alienation and overall loss is intensified by the weaning, which is the decisive separation between child and mother. The child's (emotional) hunger for the milk of love, which was generously given to him only lately, can then become unbearable, and he feels betrayed by his mother, who can be perceived by him as a threatening, hostile figure. Kakar suggests that this terrible weaning experience is connected with the myth (mentioned earlier) of Pūtanā, who tries to kill the infant Kṛṣṇa with her poisoned breasts (1978, p. 147).

A further cause of the perception of women as powerful and terrible beings, according to Obeyesekere (1984, p. 439), is the fact that the woman's repressed aggressive drive tends to be expressed towards her child, whenever he frustrates her, since he is the only object to whom her rage can be safely directed. Further, there are occasions when she seems to be remote and unapproachable, especially during her periods, when she is considered polluted and rendered 'untouchable' according to the Brahmanical values (Carstairs 1957, p. 158). Thus, the untouchable, menstruating mother must also reinforce the child's perception of the frightening, violent mother (the most relevant goddess here being Kālī).

I now summarize chapter 14, which has looked at our anthropological, psychoanalytical, and folklore-related material. It has been seen that the creative, life-giving power of women has long been acknowledged in India, probably even since the time of the Indus Valley Civilization. The great power of women, however, is not always regarded as auspicious. Rather, our material has shown that the feminine power's dangerous, destructive, and hostile nature—which makes this power complicated—is fully acknowledged in both aboriginal/Dravidian and Brahmanical traditions. Our data on the Brahmanical perception of women has been especially informative as regards how the perception of women as powerful and complex beings may have arisen.

## 15. SUPPORTING MATERIAL FOR THE IDEA THAT FEMININE POWER AND COMPLEXITY LEAD TO HER SPLITTING AND MULTIPLYING

In the preceding two chapters (13 & 14), I have presented literary and non-literary (viz. anthropological, psychoanalytical, etc.) material attesting to the Indian perception of women as powerful and complex beings. So far, however, we have not really explained the connection between the powerful and complex feminine principle and the multiplicity of the feminine. In the present chapter, therefore, I would like to point out some material that will support the idea that the power and complexity of the feminine lead to her splitting and multiplying.

Before we proceed, however, we may note in passing that this idea, in the main, may also be relevant to male multiplicity as well. Where male multiplicity occurs, the notion of power and complexity often seems to be present.[7] As I said in the introduction to this study, however, the occurrences of male multiplicity in Hinduism are

---

[7] The Rudras (often eleven in number) are a case in point (Mani 1975, pp. 654–55). The *Viṣṇu Parāṇa* (1.5.41–43), for instance, says that when they were created by Śiva, they threatened to eat him (cited in O'Flaherty 1976, p. 30). In other Purāṇic myths, the Rudras are described as born of Brahmā's anger; as terrible and destructive and ruining the universe; as giving Dakṣa an evil disposition; as turning into anger, injury, old age, etc. (ibid.). The Rudras thus seem to be associated with various chthonic powers. Another relevant example is the powerful Asuras who multiply through their blood dropping on the ground, e.g. Raktabīja (DM 8.39ff) and Andhaka (*Vāmana Purāṇa* 43; *Viṣṇudharmottara Purāṇa* 1.226.1–82; summarized in O'Flaherty 1973, pp. 281–82). The multiple Kauravas of the Mbh may also be noted as a good example here. They, and especially Duryodhana, are regarded as possessing great evil powers (Mani 1975, pp. 257–63, 399–40).

insignificant compared with those of feminine multiplicity and are, therefore, not included in this study.

## 15.1 SPLIT INTO TWO

We now look at material that points to the idea that feminine power and complexity result in the splitting and multiplying of the feminine. We begin by considering the splitting of the feminine into two.

We saw in chapter 14 that the Hindus have two contrasting images of the feminine: the conscious ideal of wifely and maternal virtue, purity, and fidelity; and the hidden perception of women as just the opposite, lustful, rampant, treacherous, etc. The conflicting forces represented by these two images of the feminine—one creative, harmonious, and maternal and the other destructive, dangerous, and erotic—are, in fact, contained in a single female. Yet, the Brahmanical values prevent the Hindu female from behaving in a manner that would incorporate these two contrasting forces, for a Hindu wife has to be an epitome of the first of the two forces (she is enjoined to be unassertive, submissive, loyal, etc.) and *cannot* have any of the second force.

In some traditions, a girl after puberty is often considered a locus of dangerous power—indicative of the second force—and, in fact, is not seen as having much of the first force until she gets married. But once she is married, she gains the first force but loses the second.

As far as the Hindu perception of women is concerned, then, the two contrasting forces of the feminine cannot exist together. These must be separate from each other. The feminine, thus, is either maternal or erotic, creative or destructive, benevolent or violent, etc. In other words, the feminine is split into two. Perhaps, that is why, as O'Flaherty points out, Indian goddesses can be divided roughly into two distinct categories, one bountiful, auspicious, and fertile, and the other erotic and dangerous (1980, pp. 90–91).

Let us look at some specific examples of splitting into two. The most explicit case is the myth (appearing in several Purāṇas—O'Flaherty 1976, p. 350) of the Goddess who, after being teased by Śiva about her dark skin, practises asceticism until she sloughs off her skin. She is then called Gaurī ('the golden one') and is now ready to get married to Śiva, while her black skin becomes the terrible goddess Kālī ('the black one').

Saṃjñā, the wife of the sun (Vivasvat), also splits into two in a Vedic myth (ibid., p. 349). One figure is Saṃjñā herself, the bright image, and the other is an identical goddess that she creates, called Chāyā ('dark shadow'). The 'dark shadow' mistreats her stepson and curses him to lose his leg. Here we have the splitting of a goddess into the good and bad mother. Another example is found in a South Indian tale of Reṇukā, though this story is not as straightforward:

> Reṇukā (whose name may mean 'more of light') was the mother of Paraśurāma; one day she became unchaste and, at the behest of his father, Paraśurāma beheaded Reṇukā; at the same time, he beheaded a dark-skinned, low-caste woman. Paraśurāma pleaded with his father to revive Reṇukā; given permission at last, the boy went in the dark and revived both bodies, but accidentally he placed the wrong head on each body. The woman with Reṇukā's head was accepted as Reṇukā; the other became a Mātaṅgī, a low-caste woman (Elmore 1913, pp. 101–02, as sum-

marized in O'Flaherty 1976, p. 351).

Thus, though not without any external aid, Reṇukā does split—upon the intrusion of the unpermissible unchasteness into her position as wife—into the dark and the light, the low- and the high-caste figures.

## 15.2 SPLIT INTO MORE THAN TWO

From the notion of splitting into two, it does not take a great deal of development to arrive at the notion of splitting into three or more. Often a female is regarded by the Hindus as possessing, not just two, but multiple different forces or categories simultaneously. As we have seen, a female is regarded as inherently complex. Thus a goddess is often split into several or more figures to represent different forces that exist within her nature. As Shulman says, 'Myths divide her into parts in an effort to deal with these conflicting attributes' (1980, p. 351).

Let us look at some examples to illustrate how feminine power and complexity lead to feminine multiplicity. A straightforward example is the *yoginīs* of the nine enclosures of the Śrī-Cakra. As we have seen in an earlier chapter, these goddesses are really manifestations of the central Goddess and are there to represent her various powers and forms.

The description of one form of the Khecarī Cakra of Sixty-four Yoginīs, as set forth in the *Matottara Tantra* (summarized by Dehejia 1986, pp. 44–45), also provides a good example of feminine multiplication resulting from her power and complexity. This cakra includes successive concentric layers of lotus petals numbering twelve, twenty-four, thirty-two, and then sixty-four. First, the twelve fearsome Yoginīs of glowing colours, decorated with a variety of ornaments, are produced from the Goddess's desire to create. Each has enough power to raise the dead and bestow all the *siddhis* on the practitioner. The twelve Yoginīs' agitation gives rise to a circle of twenty-four Yoginīs of great potency, each having different appearance and a distinct *vāhana*. The lotus then expands into a circle of thirty-two Yoginīs, who can assume any form they desire and have varying weapons as well as mounts. They are intoxicated with their own power. Their power and joy result in the fully blown lotus of Sixty-four Yoginīs, who have various colours and mounts. All are four-armed, hold weapons, and are adorned with jewels.

The next example is Lalitā Parameśvarī, who is powerful enough to kill the great Asuras (*Lalitā-māhātmya* 31.21) and is praised as the ocean of eternal wisdom. According to the *Lalitā-māhātmya*, she 'divides herself into sixteen (distinct forms) for the sake of protecting the universe' (31.11; tr. Tagare 1984, p. 1228). Sixteen are the centres of the sacred spots scattered throughout the universe, and there Lalitā Parameśvarī in her sixteen forms will stay (ibid. 31.9ff). The Ten Mahāvidyās, too, come into being when Satī, upon losing her temper and assuming a dreadful form, multiplies herself into ten forms, as we have seen above. The ten distinct forms of Satī represent different powers and features of Satī and completely surround and frighten Śiva (Kinsley 1986, pp. 162–63).

The Gadaba myth of the origin of witches describes the splitting of the rich and powerful goddess Birkamdai, who lent money to the gods and ghosts, many of whom worked in her house.

> When she was about to die, she instructed her servants to cut her body into small pieces, put the pieces into a pot,

> and float it down the river. … A Gadaba woman fished out the vessel. … She ate some on the spot and took some home. She had seven granddaughters. They feasted on the meat and the result was that they became the first witches (quoted in Harper 1977, p. 59).

Thus, the goddess's power did not perish even in death and, instead, split and multiplied into chthonic forms as witches.

The following story (noted earlier) from the Baiga of Rewa State in the Central Provinces describes how the power generated through anger stemming from injustice suffered by a female resulted in her multiplication.

> A new bride named Piri Deshahi was enraged when her husband seduced one of her seven sisters on their wedding night. As a result of her anger, she gave birth to twenty-one daughters who were responsible for all the diseases which plague man and cattle (ibid., pp. 59–60).

Sometimes, feminine multiplicity might, at first, appear to be connected only with feminine power, and not with her complexity; rarely, however, does feminine multiplication result only from feminine power entirely free from complexity and ambivalence. The following Purāṇic myth illustrates this point well:

> The demon Ruru with his army attacked the gods, who sought refuge with Devī. She laughed, and an army of goddesses emerged from her mouth. They killed Ruru and his army, but then they were hungry and asked for food.

> Devī summoned Rudra Paśupati and said, 'You have the form of a goat and you smell like a goat. These ladies will eat your flesh or else they will eat everything, even me'. Śiva said, '... let the goddesses eat that which pregnant women have defiled with their touch, and newborn children, and women who cry all the time'. Devī refused this disgusting food, and finally Śiva said, 'I will give you something never tasted by anyone else: the two balls resembling fruits below my navel. Eat the testicles that hang there and be satisfied' (tr. O'Flaherty 1973, p. 280).

Feminine complexity here even involves the castration of a male.

The myth of *śakti-pīṭha* may also be interpreted as indicative of the feminine power of anger (in this case Satī's anger caused by Dakṣa not inviting Śiva or Satī to the sacrifice) resulting in feminine multiplicity. There are numerous variations of this myth (Earndl 1987, pp. 58ff), but relevant to us are the following. First, some later versions refer to the dead body of Satī falling bit by bit on the ground and explain that the places where pieces of her body fell are the *śakti-pīṭha* (power-seat). Some other versions, such as the one in the *Matsya Purāṇa*, do not describe the physical splitting of Satī's body but refer to various places and forms in which she is found and should be worshipped (Tiwari 1985, pp. 16–17). This could be understood as a form of splitting or multiplication. An interesting recent cult involving the *śakti-pīṭha* is that of Śerāṅvālī, who manifests herself as seven sisters who are identified with seven *pīṭha*. One of the most vigorous aspects of this cult is pilgrimage to these sacred places (Earndl 1987, p. 71). These places are considered extremely potent, and so 'pilgrimage is efficacious' (ibid., p. 75). Also interesting is a recent phenomenon noted by Earndl in connection with these *pīṭha* that points clearly to the process of the multiplying of the feminine actually taking place:

> There is no finite limit to the number of pilgrimage places or to the number of goddess manifestations. New places are always cropping up ... (ibid., p. 72).

My last example of splitting is that feminine power which manifests as Speech. In the Vedic hymn 10.125, her power is said to have given 'birth to the father on the head of this world' (verse 7); to 'spread out over all creatures and touch the very sky with the crown of my head' (ibid.); to 'embrace all creatures' (verse 8) (for whoever eats food, truly sees, breathes, hears, does so through her, and thus all dwell in her—verse 4); to pervade sky and earth (verse 6); and to 'make him [whom she loves] a sage, a wise man, a Brahmin' (verse 5). Her power also not only enables Rudra's arrow to strike down the hater of prayer, but incites 'the contest among the people' (verse 6). She is said—as can be expected from the very nature of speech (composed of different phonemic units)—to have been divided up into various parts and to dwell in many places and in many forms (verse 3).

We have looked at some examples that illustrate the idea that feminine power and complexity lead to her splitting and multiplication. We may also mention here that there are many instances of feminine multiplicity that do not explicitly involve the 'splitting' of the feminine but that, nevertheless, could be interpreted as presupposing some form of multiplication of the feminine resulting from her complexity and power. These instances support the notion that just one image is far from enough—and a great many images are needed—to represent the extraordinary power, the richness of characteristics, and the complexity of the feminine. I am referring to such large groups of females as the host of mothers described in chapter 46 of the *Śalya Parva* of the Mbh (the text names 192 but says that there are many more besides), who have extremely strong characteristics as well as great power; the 360 Śaktis inhabiting the six Cakras mentioned in chapter 32 of the *Lalitā-māhātmya*; and the 144 Kālīs envisaged in some form of the worship of the Wheel of the Twelve Kālīs (Pandey 1963, p. 521). Regarding the *Śalya Parva*'s mothers, it has often been argued that they were adopted from the aboriginal/Dravidian goddess worship, and this is correct with regard to many of them. But not all the mothers mentioned there are accounted for by this interpretation, for, as Tiwari (1985, pp. 4, 18) suggests, quite a few of the names may be purely *ad hoc*, artificial creations that do not refer to real goddesses. Nor is this historical derivation of this host of mothers from actual sources likely to account for the enormous size of this group, for we have here, not just the 192 mothers that are named, but also 'many other mothers … numbering *by thousands*' (tr. Ganjuli 1981, p. 129). These two aspects of this group of mothers—viz. the artificial creation of many goddess names and the immense size of this group—could well be the results of profuse feminine multiplication boosted by feminine power and complexity.

Lastly, it is worth noting that the increasingly greater intensification of feminine multiplication may lead to a situation in which one cannot help regarding *all* women as one's mother. In other words, the mother, because of her power and complexity, may multiply herself to such a degree that she is found everywhere throughout the world. Mythology supplies several instances of regarding all women as one's mother (O'Flaherty 1973, pp. 51, 63, 190–91, 201, 204, 211). To give just one example, we may mention the story of Skanda in which he tries to make love to the wives of the gods but, in every woman he summons, he sees his mother's form and, eventually, becomes passionless, thinking, 'The universe is filled with my mother' (ibid., p. 204).

In chapters 12 to 15, I have examined two explanations of feminine multiplicity based on the Hindu perception of women. One is that feminine multiplicity results from a demeaning perception of women. The other says that the real cause of feminine multiplicity is feminine power and complexity. The results of our discussions indicate that feminine multiplicity is not so much the result of the demeaning, male chauvinistic perception of women as the inevitable solution to the problem of coping with the Hindu perception of women as powerful and complex beings. One image was not enough. The feminine had to be split. Such is the complexity and power of the feminine that she must be seen in multiplicity to represent her full implications.

# 16. ACTUAL HUMAN EXPERIENCE OF HAVING MULTIPLE MOTHERS

This chapter will briefly explore yet another plausible explanation—again based on the Hindu perception of women—of feminine multiplicity. This explanation and the preceding explanation—which involved the idea that feminine power and complexity result in multiplicity—do not have to be regarded as mutually exclusive.

The present explanation is derived from actual human experience in which a Hindu child is looked after by multiple females who are all perceived by the child as 'mothers'. In addition to the real mother herself, there are, for instance, elder sisters, who 'are expected, from an early age, to take a share in looking after their younger brothers and sisters' (Carstairs 1957, p. 71). The number of these sisters may not be small in joint families, in which many Indians live (Obeyesekere 1984, p. 435), because all the young women of a person's own lineage are considered sisters (Carstairs 1957, p. 70). The close relationship of a child with the sisters is probably reinforced by the fact that, unlike the real mother, the sisters are not required to refrain from expressing their love for the child outwardly in the presence of the grandparents (ibid., p. 71). This holds true of the child's relationship with any female (other than the real mother) who acts as 'mother'. In a joint family, there are also other women who look after the child, e.g. the aunts.

Significantly, these females who take part in looking after the child are not simply *perceived* as 'mothers' but, often, also *referred to* as 'mothers'—which probably reinforces the perception of them as mothers. In Tamilnadu, for instance, the term *amma* ('mother') can be applied to, not only one's own mother, but also to persons in the category of mother, e.g. mother's sister (Trawick 1990, p. 113). This term, in fact, could be applied to many other people (ibid.). It is also significant that, in the joint family, parents' love is not focused only on their own child but consciously redirected to others' children. In a Tamil family studied by Trawick, for instance, 'mothers deliberately spurned or mistreated their own children, forcing their own and their children's affection away from the closest blood bond' (ibid., p. 103). All this, then, enables many children to grow up with more than one 'mother' in India. For example, Jnana Oli, one of the children in Trawick's Tamil family,

> had a plurality of mother. Many laps cradled him, many hands fed him. He slipped without friction in and out among them as though they were all interchangeable. And they themselves aimed to be equally loving toward him and all the other children of the house … (ibid., p. 229).

The sharing of children among women may take place also between different households, and this seems to be an ancient custom in Tamilnadu (ibid., p. 155). There, it is common, says Trawick, for a woman to 'take into her house the child or children of one of her kinswomen and raise them as her own for a time' (ibid., p. 156). This system of foster motherhood enables children to experience not only more than one 'mother' but also more than one household as home.

Some scholars suggest, further, that, even in the pre-Aryan period, some societies in India were organized in such a way that multiple mothers possessed a child-in-common while it did not matter who the father was (Kosambi 1950, esp. pp. 70–80). Citing many references, from the Vedas, to males having multiple mothers,[8] Kosambi argues that these represent an ancient custom of group-marriage which is characterized by a single child having many mothers. In chapter 2 of the present study, I considered Vedic female heptads—such as the Seven Mothers of Soma and Agni—as having a symbolic meaning because of the magic number seven, which evidently is a very special number in the Vedas. Kosambi interprets Soma's and Agni's Seven Mothers, as well as many other instances of multiple mothers[9] having a child-in-common, as reflecting an actual family structure. If Kosambi is right, then we may say that the concept of the Seven Mothers of Soma and Agni was patterned after an actual human experience of having multiple mothers as well as imbued with the symbolic meaning and value contained in the number seven.

It has been seen, in this chapter, that there exists in India an actual human experience of growing up with multiple mothers. I have also indicated that such an experience may have existed even in ancient times. It may be that such an experience has made a contribution to the formation of many groups of multiple mother-goddesses in India.

---

[8] Often multiple mothers are indicated by multiple heads (like the Kārttikeya), faces, or mouths of the male (child).

[9] Many of them are not seven in number.

# CONCLUSION

By way of conclusion, I shall summarize the foregoing discussions and suggest a way to explain Hindu feminine multiplicity as a whole based on the results of our discussions.

In Part I, which dealt with some of the representative groups of multiple goddesses individually, we considered the meanings of feminine multiplicity within the context of each individual group. The results of Part I have already been recapitulated in chapter 11 at the beginning of Part II, and I shall not repeat the same summary here, other than saying the following. The two main ideas that we came up with regarding the symbolic meaning of feminine multiplicity involved in the groups that we considered were: the idea of renewal (cyclic or spiritual), which means a return to an original point, which is again a new beginning of another unfolding process; and the idea of the emanation of the One as the manifold and the withdrawal of the manifold back into the One. These two ideas both seem to recognize the process of *unfolding* from an Origin as well as the reverse process of *return* to the Origin. These processes—which are really understood as two aspects of one process—are expressed through various means, depending on the group of females: e.g. through the intrinsically powerful number seven, through astronomical and other natural phenomena, through a form of linguistic cosmology (e.g. in the case of the letters, *mātṛkās*), and so on. Part I, however, left several questions unanswered, such as 'Why is it the *feminine* that multiplies?'

Part II, then, sought to answer such questions and to explain feminine multiplicity in Hinduism on the basis of the particularly Indian perception of women by drawing on evidence derived from literary material and from anthropological, psychoanalytical, and folklore-related data. It has been seen that the prominence of feminine multiplicity in India is not so much the result of the officially sanctioned demeaning, male chauvinistic perception of women—which says that women are all the same, that they cannot do anything alone, and that multiple women are required to match one man—as the consequence of having to deal with the hidden perception, on the part of many Hindus, of the feminine as being extremely powerful (sexually, magically, etc.) and complex and far from subservient to the masculine; she contains within herself a variety of different, often conflicting, forces that may be unpredictable, destructive, and dangerous. Thus, the feminine had to be split, for her power and complexity is so great that she must be seen, not in one image, but in multiplicity to represent her full implications. This splitting involves the fact that the Brahmanical values, which enjoin modest, wifely virtues on the Hindu woman, would not allow the other kinds of forces to coexist within her.

Another of our explanations of feminine multiplicity based on the Hindu perception of women is that since there is an actual human experience of growing up with more than one 'mother' in Hindu joint families and, possibly, in an ancient family system of group-marriage, the concept of a group of multiple mother-goddesses is not in the least alien to the Hindus. It is probable that this experience of having multiple mothers has played a role in the formation of the concept of groups of goddesses.

We have to remember, however, that these explanations based on the Hindu perception of women, by themselves, are not sufficient to account exhaustively for the multiplicity of the feminine in India. We need also to take into consideration the astronomical, numerical, linguistic-cosmological, and other ways in which the Hindus have perceived their relationship with nature. It would appear, then, that we cannot fully appreciate feminine multiplicity in India without understanding all these various aspects of Hindu culture and thought.

Lastly, I should like to propose to combine the explanations yielded by Parts I and II in a slightly more unified manner. As mentioned above, the central notion in Part I is that of unfolding from an Origin and return to the Origin. Basing ourselves on this notion, we may say that the worship of a group of multiple goddesses may be understood as the veneration of the universe as the Origin which unfolds itself in a variety of forms, each of the forms being no mere illusion but energy-matter (*śakti*) that partakes of the reality and divinity of the Origin, which can return all those forms back into itself. The worshipper in this cosmology is inevitably a part of the activities of the Origin, as indicated in many of the sections of Part I entitled 'Mode and aim of worship/other practice'. Part I, however, did not specify that this Origin had to be female, or why so. On the basis of Part II, however, we may say that the Origin appears as a variety of forms *precisely* because this Origin is a female—often seen as the mother—whose power and complexity bursts forth as multiple forms. The masculine, on the other hand, is so uncomplicated (compared with the feminine) that he should have no need to multiply. Or rather, he cannot multiply; he does not have the power to multiply, as she does. The feminine inherently contains immense power and is incomprehensibly complex—she is an all-embracing amalgam of various, often conflicting, forces, creative and destructive, benevolent and violent, harmonious and chaotic, etc. Thus, not only is the Origin most capable of appearing as the manifold, but she *necessarily* manifests herself as the manifold because her complexity and power would not permit her to remain 'one' in the Brahmanical universe. Further, her complexity and power would not, otherwise, have allowed the worshipper to relate to, understand, or come to terms with this Original Feminine, from whom he cannot in fact separate himself.

This perspective seems to place greater emphasis on the *unfolding* side of the Origin's activity than on the *return* side, whereas the perspective provided by Part I may be said to be slightly more concerned with the returning of the manifold to the One Origin than with the unfolding side. For example, the Twelve Kālīs (Flood 1988, pp. 159ff) are a case in point. Soteriologically, in this Part-I perspective, the return to the Origin—i.e. the full realization that all are emanations of, and contained within, the One Origin—*is* even the ultimate aim itself, though the Origin is, again, a new beginning of another unfolding process.

One might wonder how the Part-II perspective works soteriologically. The answer seems to be that the 'splitting' (or multiplication) of the feminine *is* itself the soteriological solution, for the ultimate problem from which the Hindus are to be saved (speaking from this perspective) is that a Hindu—who is conditioned by the Brahmanical values which enjoin certain qualities on women (and men)—cannot cope with certain real (as opposed to ideal) women, especially mothers, who seem to become so powerful and so complex precisely because of such Brahmanical values and yet do not fit in with these same values. In order to enable such a Hindu to appreciate and understand the whole of such a woman, what is required is her 'splitting and multiplying', which serves to represent her full implications. Further, having multiple mothers, and not just one mother, is quite a natural thing in this culture since many Hindus grow up with many 'mothers'. Thus, from this perspective, the manifested state (as opposed to the unmanifested one Origin) itself brings the state of salvation to those who are conditioned, consciously or unconsciously, by the above-mentioned Brahmanical values. However, once such conditioning disappears totally from the practitioner, it would seem that the soteriology of the return to the Origin would also become quite relevant. If it is objected to this that I have said that having multiple mothers is a natural condition for the Hindus, then it is to be noted that even those who are looked after by multiple mothers will, as they grow up, become more and more conscious that one of these caretakers is, in fact, their real mother.

At any rate, whichever perspective the worshipper is more inclined towards, his or her worship seems to be an attempt to live in harmony with the wonder of creation, the display of activities of the *one*, original, powerful Feminine, who is simultaneously conceived of *in multiplicity*.

## BIBLIOGRAPHY


Agrawala, V. S. 1963. *The Glorification of the Great Goddess*. Varanasi: All-India Kashiraj Trust.

Alper, Harvey P. 1989. 'The Cosmos as Śiva's Language-Game: "Mantra" According to Kṣemarāja's *Śivasūtravimarśinī*' in Alper (ed.) 1989.

____________. (ed.). 1989. *Mantra*. Albany: State University of New York Press.

Archer, W. G. 1974. *The Hill of Flutes: Life, Love and Poetry in Tribal India—A Portrait of the Santals*. London: George Allen & Unwin Ltd.

Aryan, K. C. 1980. The Little Goddesses (*Mātrikās*). New Delhi: Rekha Prakashan.

Babb, Lawrence A. 1975. *The Divine Hierarchy: Popular Hinduism in Central India*. New York: Columbia University Press.

Banerjea, Jitendra Nath. 1956. *The Development of Hindu Iconography*. New Delhi: Munshiram Manoharlal Publishers Pvt. Ltd. Reprinted 1974.

Beane, Wendell Charles. 1977. *Myth, Cult and Symbols in Śakta Hinduism: A Study of the Indian Mother Goddess*. Leiden: E. J. Brill.

Beck, Brenda E. F. 1981. 'The Goddess and the Demon. A Local South Indian Festival and Its Wider Context' in Madeleine Biardeau (ed.), *Autour de la Déesse Hindoue*. Paris: École des Hautes Études en Sciences Sociales, pp. 83–136.

Bhandarkar, R. G. 1913. *Vaiṣṇavism, Śaivism, and Minor Religious Systems*. Strassburg: K. J. Trubner. Reprinted by Garland Publishing, Inc. New York, 1980.

Bhattacharyya, Narendra Nath. 1974 (1973). *History of the Śākta Religion*. New Delhi: Munshiram Manoharlal Publishers Pvt. Ltd.

Brooks, Douglas Renfrew. 1987. 'The Śrīvidyā School of Śākta Tantrism: A Study of the Texts and Contexts of the Living Tradition in South India'. Ph.D. diss., Harvard University.

Brubaker, Richard L. 1978. 'The Ambivalent Mistress: A Study of South Indian Village Goddesses and Their Religious Meaning'. Ph.D. diss.,

University of Chicago.

_________________. 1979. 'Barbers, Washermen, and Other Priests: Servants of the South Indian Village and Its Goddess' in *History of Religions*, Vol. 19, No. 2, pp. 128–52.

Bryson, Reid A. 1989. 'Environmental Opportunities and Limits for Development' in *Environmental Conservation*, Vol. 16. No. 4, pp. 299–305. Published by The Foundation for Environmental Conservation.

Bühler, G. (tr.). 1886. *The Laws of Manu.* (=*Sacred Books of the East*, Vol. XXV. ed. F. Max Müller). Reprinted 1964 by Motilal Banarsidass, Delhi.

Campbell, Joseph. 1962. *The Masks of God: Oriental Mythology*. British ed. published 1973 by Souvenir Press Ltd., London.

Carstairs, G. M. 1957. *The Twice-Born: A Study of a Community of High-Caste Hindus*. London: The Hogarth Press.

Coburn, Thomas B. 1984. *Devī-Māhātmya: The Crystallization of the Goddess Tradition*. Delhi: Motilal Banarsidass.

Coomaraswamy, Ananda K. 1980. *Yakṣas*, 2nd ed. New Delhi: Munshiram Manoharlal Publishers Pvt. Ltd.

Crooke, W. 1896. *The Popular Religion and Folk-lore of Northern India*, 2nd ed., Vol. 1. Delhi: Munshiram Manoharlal Publishers Pvt. Ltd..

Danielou, Alain. 1964. *Hindu Polytheism*. New York: Pantheon Books.

Das, H. C. 1981. *Tantricism: A Study of the Yoginī Cult*. New Delhi: Stering Publishers Pvt. Ltd.

Dehejia, Vidya. 1986. *Yoginī Cult and Temples: A Tantric Tradition*. New Delhi: National Museum.

Dube, S. C. 1955. *Indian Village*. London: Routledge & Kegan Paul Ltd.

Dyczkowski, Mark, S. G. 1987. *The Doctrine of Vibration*. Albany: State University of New York Press.

Earndl, Kathleen Marie. 1987. 'Victory to the Mother: The Goddess Cult of Northwest India'. Ph.D. diss., University of Wisconsin-Madison.

Eggeling, Julius. (tr.). 1882. *The Śatapatha-Brāhmaṇa According to the Text of the Madhyandina School*, Part 1. (=*Sacred Books of the*

*East*, Vol. XII. ed. F. Max Müller). Reprinted 1963 by Motilal Banarsidass, Delhi.

Eliade, Mireea. 1954. *The Myth of the Eternal Return: Or, Cosmos and History*. Princeton: Princeton University Press.

_________. 1958. *Yoga: Immortality and Freedom*. New York: Bollingen Foundation Inc.

Elmore, W. T. 1913. *Dravidian Gods in Modern Hinduism*. Reprinted by Asian Educational Services, New Delhi, 1984.

Elwin, Verrier. 1969. *The Nagas in the Nineteenth Century*. Bombay: Oxford University Press.

Fawcett, F. 1890. 'On Some Festivals to Village Goddesses' in *Journal of the Anthropological Society of Bombay*, Vol. 2, pp. 261–82.

Finn, Louise M. (intro., tr., & annot.). 1986. *The Kulacūḍāmaṇi Tantra and The Vāmakeśvara Tantra with the Jayaratha Commentary*. Wiesbaden: Otto Harrassowitz.

Flood, Gavin D. 1988. 'Consciousness Embodied: A Study in the Monistic Śaivism of Kashmir'. Ph.D. diss., University of Lancaster.

Frazer, Sir James George. 1933. *The Golden Bough: A Study in Magic and Religion*, 3rd ed., Part V: *Spirits of the Corn and the Wild*, Vol. 1. London: Macmillan & Co. Ltd. First published 1912.

Freed, Ruth S., & Freed, Stanley A. 1962. 'Two Mother Goddess Ceremonies of Delhi State in the Great and Little Traditions' in *Southwestern Journal of Anthropology*, Vol. 18, pp. 246–77.

Ganguli , Kisari Mohan. (tr.). 1981. *The Mahābhārata*, 4th ed. New Delhi: Munshiram Manoharlal Publishers Pvt. Ltd.

Gimbutas, Marija. 1989. *The Language of the Goddess*. San Francisco: Harper & Row.

Goudriaan, T. 1979. 'Introduction, History and Philosophy' in Gupta, et al. (1979).

_________. 1981. 'Hindu Tantric Literature in Sanskrit' in T. Goudriaan and S. Gupta, *Hindu Tantric and Śākta Literature*, which is Vol. 2, Fasc. 2, of Jan Gonda (ed.) *A History of Indian Literature*, Wiesbaden: Otto Harrassowitz.

Griffith, Ralph T. H. (tr.). 1963. *The Hymns of the Ṛgveda*, 4th ed., two vols. Varanasi: Chowkhamba Sanskrit Series Office.

Guha, J. P. 1967. *Seals and Statuettes of Kulli, Zhob, Mohenjo Daro and Harappa*. New Delhi: Associated Publishing House.

Gupta, Sanjukta. 1979. 'Modes of Worship and Meditation' in Gupta et al. (1979).

Gupta, Sanjukta, et al. 1979. *Hindu Tantrism*. Leiden: E. J. Brill.

Harper, Katherine Anne. 1977. 'An Iconological Study of the Origins and Development of the Saptamātṛkās'. Ph.D. diss., University of California, Los Angeles.

Hastings, James (ed.). 1917. *Encyclopaedia of Religion and Ethics*, Vol. 9. Edinburgh: T. & T. Clark.

Hawley, John Stratton, & Wulff, Donna Marie. (eds.). 1982. *The Divine Consort: Rādhā and the Goddesses of India*. Berkeley: Graduate Theological Union.

Hazra, R. C. 1975. *Studies in the Purāṇic Records on Hindu Rites and Customs*, 2nd ed. Delhi: Motilal Banarsidass.

Hiltebeitel, Alf. 1978. 'The Indus Valley "Proto-Śiva", Reexamined Through Reflections on the Goddess, the Buffalo, and the Symbolism of *vāhanas*' in the *Anthropos* 73, pp. 767–81.

__________. 1980. 'Rāma and Gilgamesh: The Sacrifices of the Water Buffalo and the Bull of Heaven' in *History of Religions*, Vol. 19, No. 3, pp. 187–224.

__________. 1988. *The Cult of Draupadī, Vol. I—Mythologies: From Gingee to Kurukṣetra*. Chicago: University of Chicago Press.

Hoens, Dirk Jan. 1979. 'Transmission and Fundamental Constituents of the Practice' in Gupta et al. (1979).

Kakar, Sudhir. 1978. *The Inner World: A Psycho-analytic Study of Childhood and Society in India*. Delhi: Oxford University Press.

Kane, Pandurang. 1974. *History of Dharmaśāstra*, Vol. II, Part II, & Vol. V, Part I, 2nd ed. Poona: Bhandarkar Oriental Research Institute.

Keith, Arthur Berriedale. (tr.). 1914. *The Veda of the Black Yajur School Entitled Taittirīya Sanhitā*. Delhi: Motilal Banarsidass.

__________. 1971. *The Religion and Philosophy of the Veda and Upanishads*, 2 vols. Westport: Greenwood Press. Originally published 1925 by Harvard University Press.

Kinsley, David. 1986. *Hindu Goddesses: Visions of the Divine Feminine in the Hindu Religious Tradition*. Berkeley: University of California

Press.
Kosambi, D. D. 1950. 'The Origin of the Brahmin Gotras' in *Journal of the Bombay Branch of the Royal Asiatic Society*, Vol. 26, pp. 21–80.

__________. 1962. *Myth and Reality: Studies in the Formation of Indian Culture*. Bombay: Popular Prakashan.

Kramrisch, Stella. 1975. 'The Indian Great Goddess' in *History of Religions*, Vol. 14, No. 4, pp. 235–65.

Kumar, Pushpendra. 1974. *Śakti Cult in Ancient India*. Varanasi: Bhartiya Publishing House.

Lévi-Strauss, Claude. 1970. *The Raw and the Cooked: Introduction to a Science of Mythology: I*. London: Jonathan Cape. First English version published 1969 by Harper & Row.

Lorenzen, David N. 1972. *The Kāpālikas and Kālāmukhas: Two Lost Śaivite Sects*. New Delhi: Thomson Press (India) Ltd.

MacDonell, Arthur Anthony, & Keith, Arthur Berriedale. 1967. *Vedic Index of Names and Subjects*, Vol. I. Delhi: Motilal Banarsidass. First ed: 1912

Mackay, Ernest. 1935. *The Indus Civilization*. London: Lovat Dickson and Thompson Ltd.

Mani, Vettam. 1975. *Purāṇic Encyclopaedia*. Delhi: Motilal Banarsidass.

Marglin, Frederique Apffel. 1982. 'Types of Sexual Union and Their Implicit Meanings' in Hawley & Wulff (1982).

Marriott, McKim. 1955. 'Little Communities in an Indigenous Civilization' in McKim Marriott (ed.) *Village India: Studies in the Little Community*. Chicago: University of Chicago Press.

Maury, Curt. 1969. *Folk Origins of Indian Art*. New York: Columbia University Press.

Mitchiner, John E. 1982. *Traditions of the Seven Ṛṣis*. Delhi: Motilal Banarsidass.

Mode, Heinz, & Chandra, Subodh. 1985. *Indian Folk Art*. New York: Alpine Fine Arts Collection, Ltd.

Monier-Williams, Sir Monier. 1899. *Sanskrit-English Dictionary*. Oxford: Clarendon Press.

Müller, F. Max. (ed.). 1965. *The Upanishads*, Part II. Delhi: Motilal

Banarsidass. First published 1884 by Clarendon Press, Oxford.

Obeyesekere, Gananath. 1984. *The Cult of the Goddess Pattini*. Chicago: University of Chicago Press.

O'Flaherty, Wendy Doniger. 1973. *Asceticism and Eroticism in the Mythology of Śiva*. London: Oxford University Press.

__________. 1975. *Hindu Myths*. Harmondsworth: Penguin Books Ltd.

__________. 1976. *The Origins of Evil in Hindu Mythology*. Berkeley: University of California Press.

__________. 1980. *Women, Androgynes, and Other Mythical Beasts*. Chicago: University of Chicago Press.

__________. 1981. *The Rig Veda: An Anthology*. Harmondsworth: Penguin Books Ltd.

Onishi, Yoshinori. 1995. 'The Devī-Māhātmya and the Buffalo Sacrifice' in *PILC Journal of Dravidic Studies*, Vol. 5, No. 2, pp. 231–47.

Pandey, Kanti Chandra. 1963. *Abhinavagupta: An Historical and Philosophical Study*. 2nd ed. Varanasi: Chowkhamba Sanskrit Series Office.

Panikkar, Shivaji K. 1988. 'Sapta-Mātṛkā Sculptures at Ellora—An Iconological Analysis' in Parimoo et al. (ed.) 1988.

Parimoo, Ratan, et al. 1988. *Ellora Caves: Sculptures and Architecture*. New Delhi: Books & Books.

Parpola, Asko. 1985. *The Sky-Garment: A Study of the Harappan Religion and Its Relation to the Mesopotamian and Later Indian Religions*. Helsinki: The Finnish Oriental Society.

Rao, S. K. Ramachandra. 1983. *The Tantra of Śrī-Chakra*. Bangalore: Sharada Prakashan.

__________. 1989. *Śrī Chakra*. Delhi: Śrī Satguru Publications.

Rao, T. A. Gopinatha. 1914. *Elements of Hindu Iconography*, Vol. 1, 2nd ed. Republished by Paragon, New York, 1968.

Rastogi, Navjivan. 1979. *The Karma Tantricism of Kashmir*, Delhi: Motilal Banarsidass.

Roy, Sarat Chandra. 1970. *The Mundas and Their Country*. Bombay: Asia Publishing House. Originally published 1912.

Sanderson, Alexis. 1985. 'Purity and Power Among the Brahmans of Kashmir' in Michael Carrithers, Steven Collins, and Steven Lukes (eds.), *The Category of the Person*, Cambridge: Cambridge University Press.

____________. 1988. 'Śaivism and the Tantric Traditions' in Stewart Sutherland, Leslie Houlden, Peter Clarke, and Friedhelm Hardy (eds.), *The World's Religions*, London: Routledge.

Sastri, H. Krishna. 1974. *South-Indian Images of Gods and Goddesses*. Delhi: Bhartiya Publishing House.

Sastri, K. N. 1957. *New Light on the Indus Civilization*, Vol. 1. Delhi: Atman Ram and Sons.

Shulman, David Dean. 1980. *Tamil Temple Myths: Sacrifice and Divine Marriage in the South Indian Śaiva Tradition*. Princeton: Princeton University Press.

Singh, Jaideva. 1977. *Pratyabhijñāhṛdayam*, 2nd ed. Delhi: Motilal Banarsidass.

___________. 1979. *Śiva-sūtras: the Yoga of Supreme Identity*. Delhi: Motilal Banarsidass.

___________. 1980. *Spanda-kārikas: the Divine Creative Pulsation*. Delhi: Motilal Banarsidass.

Slusser, Mary Shepherd. 1982. *Nepal Maṇḍala: A Cultural Study of the Kathmandu Valley*, Vol. 1. Princeton: Princeton University Press.

Spratt, Philip. 1966. *Hindu Culture and Personality: a Psychoanalytical Study*. Bombay: Manaktalas.

Tagare, Gonesh Vasudeo (tr. & annot.). 1984. *The Brahmāṇḍa Purāṇa*, Parts IV & V. Delhi: Motilal Banarsidass.

Tiwari, J. N. 1985. *Goddess Cults in Ancient India (with Special Reference to the First Seven Centuries A.D.)*. Delhi: Sundeep Prakashan.

Trawick, Margaret. 1990. *Notes on Love in a Tamil Family*. Berkeley: University of California Press.

van Buitenen, J. A. B. 1975. *The Mahābhārata*, Vol. 2. Chicago: University of Chicago Press.

van Kooij, D. R. 1972. *Worship of the Goddess According to the Kālikāpurāṇa*, Part 1, Leiden: E. J. Brill.

Wheelock, Wade T. 1989. 'The Mantra in Vedic and Tantric Ritual' in Alper (ed.) 1989.

Whitehead, Henry. 1921. *The Village Gods of South India*. Delhi: Summit Publications. Reprinted 1976.